DEBATE Pro

Book 4

DARAKWON

Author Jonathan S. McClelland
- BA in English with a Writing Concentration, University of South Carolina, Columbia, SC, USA
- Former English instructor at Daewon Foreign Language High School
- Current debate instructor for elementary school students
- Former curriculum developer at Korean Army Intelligence School
- Expert test developer of TOEFL, TOEIC, and TEPS

DEBATE Pro Book 4

Publisher Chung Kyudo
Editors Hong Inpyo, Cho Sangik
Proofreader Michael A. Putlack
Designers Zo Hwayoun, Choi Jungeun

First Published in February 2014
By Darakwon, Inc.
Darakwon Bldg., 211, Munbal-ro, Paju-si, Gyeonggi-do 10881
Republic of Korea
Tel: 82-2-736-2031 (Ext. 250)
Fax: 82-2-732-2037

Copyright © 2014 Darakwon, Inc.

All rights reserved. No part of this publication may be reproduced, stored in a retrieval system, or transmitted in any form or by any means, electronic, mechanical, photocopying or otherwise, without the prior consent of the copyright owner. Refund after purchase is possible only according to the company regulations. Contact the above telephone number for any inquiries. Consumer damages caused by loss, damage, etc. can be compensated according to the consumer dispute resolution standards announced by the Korea Fair Trade Commission. An incorrectly collated book will be exchanged.

ISBN 978-89-277-0709-7 58740
978-89-277-0677-9 58740 (set)

www.darakwon.co.kr

Components Main Book / Workbook
13 12 11 10 9 8   25 26 27 28 29

Instilling Knowledge and Skills
for Thoughtful Debate

DEBATE Pro

Book 4

Preface

The *Debate Pro* series is designed to provide students with an intermediate EFL ability with a sound understanding of a variety of debate topics and develop their speaking, listening, and critical thinking skills through debate. The series consists of eight sets of books, each of which includes a Main Book and a Workbook. Each Main Book includes five chapters covering five debate skills. Within each chapter, there are two units which each cover different topics for a total of ten debate topics per book. The Workbook supplements the Main Book by helping students understand the topic more deeply, developing skills for making examples and doing research, and evaluating the debates. The Workbook can be used in class and for homework assignments.

In the book, every debate topic is introduced with a large color photograph relating to the topic. Students are asked to analyze the picture and formulate opinions about the topic through a series of six warm-up questions. The topic is then explained in more detail through a reading passage of about 300 words which briefly presents background information about the topic before outlining arguments in favor of and against the topic. The passages are followed by vocabulary and comprehension exercises. Students are then required to apply what they have learned from the passage to answer a series of in-depth questions relating to the debate topic. Following these questions, students are given opinion examples before learning the debate skill for each topic. Finally, students will have the chance to apply their knowledge to create a full debate with the assistance of sample arguments and a debate flow chart.

Each book provides free MP3 files with recordings of the reading passages and opinion examples for every unit. There is also a Teacher's Guide available at www.darakwon.co.kr that includes answer keys and sample answers for every unit as well as teaching tips and suggestions for supplementing the material.

The *Debate Pro* series has the following features:

- Ten different debate topics per book covering a range of themes including education, technology, relationships, and responsibility
- Reading passages which provide a general understanding of arguments both for and against the given topic
- Questions that require students to formulate arguments and supporting opinions about each topic
- Five different debate skills per book designed to improve students' critical thinking and speaking skills
- Sample opinions and argument examples which help students develop their own arguments
- Free MP3 files with recordings of all passages and sample opinions

Contents

About This Book _7

Chapter 1
Creating Expert Opinion Examples

- **Unit 01**   Outlawing Violent Sports _12
- **Unit 02**   Part-Time Jobs for Teenagers _22

Chapter 2
Creating Statistical Examples

- **Unit 03**   Teaching Practical Subjects _34
- **Unit 04**   Child Curfews _44

Chapter 3
Creating Academic Studies Examples

- **Unit 05**   Internet Censorship _56
- **Unit 06**   Free Public Transportation _66

Chapter 4
Creating Effective Rebuttals

- **Unit 07**   Punishing Parents _78
- **Unit 08**   Studying Abroad _88

Chapter 5
Creating Closing Speeches

- **Unit 09**   Universal Healthcare _100
- **Unit 10**   Nuclear Weapons _110

About This Book

Overview

Debate Pro main book consists of five chapters. Each chapter contains two units with each focusing on the same debate skill. Every unit is further subdivided into part A and part B. Part A, Learning about the Topic, introduces students to the topic of the unit and consists of approximately one hour of learning material. Part B, Debating the Topic, requires students to formulate their arguments and debate the topic of the unit. The total time required for Part B is also approximately one hour.

Introduction for each section

Warm-up

This part includes a picture related to the topic for students to analyze. The pictures are followed by six warm-up questions. The questions in Part A require students to analyze the picture and can be answered as a class. In Part B, students draw upon their knowledge about the topic to answer questions with a partner.

Reading Passage

This part consists of a single reading passage approximately 300 words in length. The passage introduces general background information about the topic and presents specific arguments with examples both in favor of and against the topic.

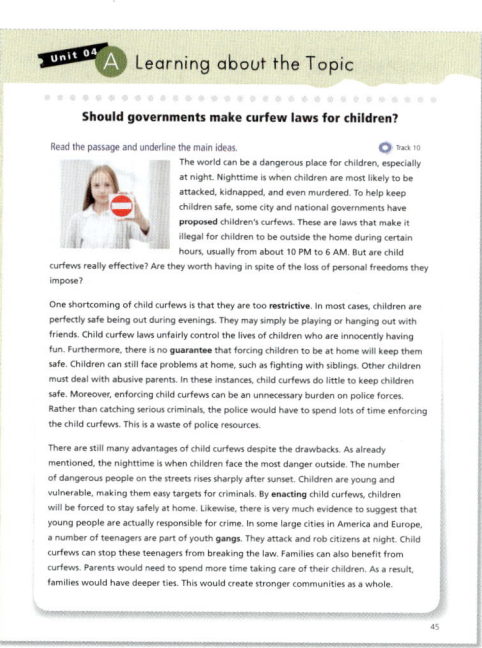

Vocabulary Check

Each reading passage is followed by five vocabulary questions to bolster students' vocabulary and ensure their understanding of the passage.

Comprehension Questions

Each reading passage includes four paired-choice reading comprehension questions. The questions ask students about the main idea of passage, factual information, and reasoning from the passage.

Questions for Debate

This portion consists of five open-ended questions related to the topic. The students must formulate opinions about each question and give reasons for their opinions. Key phrases are provided to help students improve their speaking skills.

Opinion Examples

In this section, two opinion examples for and against the topic are provided. Students are required to understand the main idea of each example opinion and its supporting arguments. They must also provide an additional argument for each opinion.

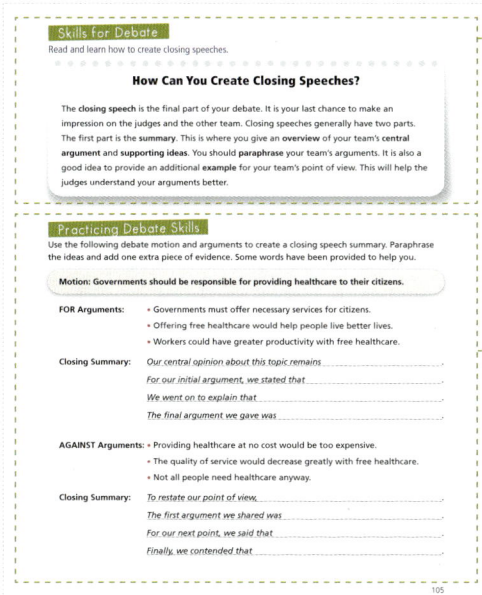

Skills for Debate

This section introduces a debate skill and explains key concepts related to the topic. Each chapter focuses on a single debate skill across two units.

Practicing Debate Skills

This exercise follows each debate skill explanation to ensure that students understand the skill and can use it during their debate.

Creating Your Debate

This section begins by introducing the skills of ARE: Argument, Reason, and Example. Following this are two sample arguments, one for PRO and one for CON, with sample notes for the ARE. On the next page are three blank columns for students to work in teams and create their AREs.

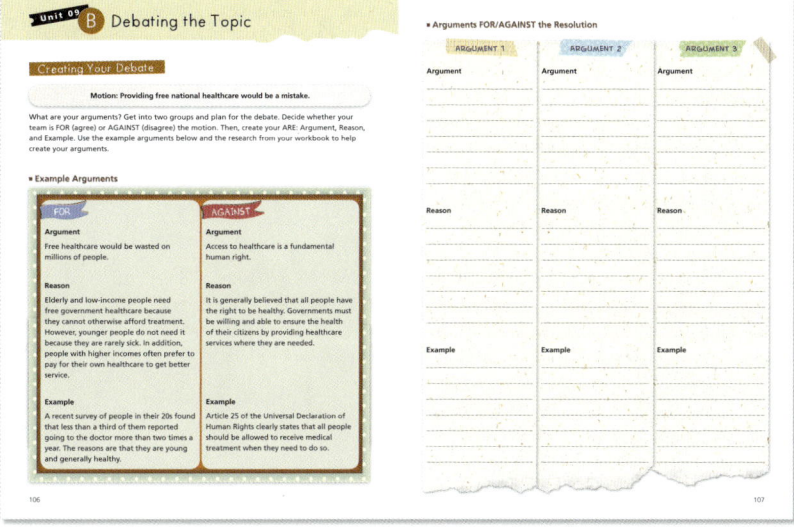

Actual Debate

This portion consists of a debate flow chart. The chart outlines the order of debate and provides sample phrases to help students use proper debate language.

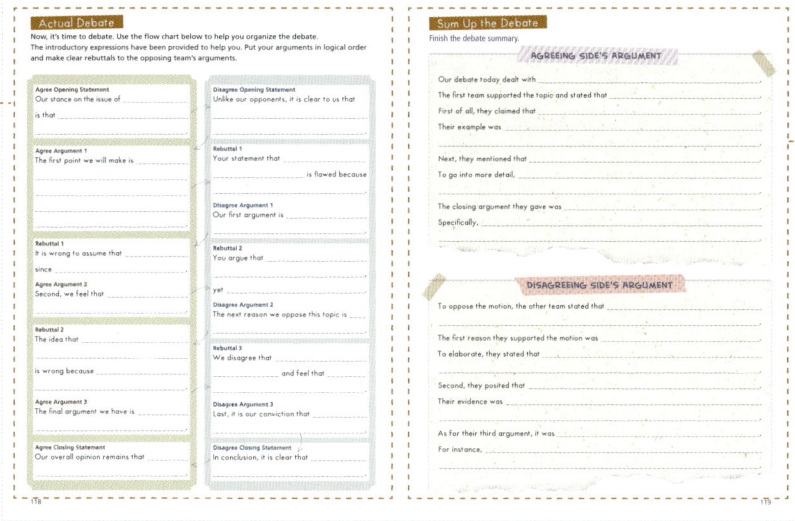

Sum Up the Debate

The final section requires students to summarize the arguments presented by both the PRO and CON teams during the debate. Sample phrases are given to help students.

Chapter 1

Creating Expert Opinion Examples

Unit 01 Outlawing Violent Sports

Unit 02 Part-Time Jobs for Teenagers

Unit 01 Outlawing Violent Sports

WARM-UP

A. Discuss the following questions as a class.

1. What do you see in the picture above?
2. What has happened to the person on the left?
3. Are the people in the picture wearing any safety equipment? If so, what?

B. Answer the following questions with a partner.

1. Can you think of any sports where the players hit each other? Name as many as you can.
2. What kinds of injuries can happen as a result of playing violent sports?
3. Do you think people should have the right to do something they know is harmful?

Unit 01　A　Learning about the Topic

Should violent sports be legal to play?

Read the passage and underline the main ideas.  Track 01

Anthony Truman was one of the most dedicated players on his high school's football team. Yet it was Anthony's love of football that ended his life. During a game, Anthony was tackled violently and received a severe head injury. He died shortly afterward at the age of 16. Although Anthony's death was tragic, it is not surprising. Sports such as football, boxing, and wrestling often result in serious bodily harm and sometimes even death. For these reasons, many are calling to make violent sports illegal to play.

The most **compelling** reason to ban violent sports is the physical injuries they cause. Sports such as boxing can easily cause permanent injuries. Consider the case of the boxer Muhammad Ali. He can barely walk and talk as a result of the head injuries he received during his boxing career. In addition, keep in mind that society already restricts other violent activities. It is illegal to attack other people in most countries. People caught fighting are very likely to be sent to jail. Since our society outlaws violent behavior, it is logical for violent sports to be restricted as well. Finally, violent sports teach children that violence is okay. Every year, the news reports about young children being injured by playing football or **imitating** wrestling moves. Banning these sports would keep children safe.

Many still believe that violent sports should be allowed to continue. Athletes should have the freedom to play violent sports if they want to. Professional football players, boxers, and wrestlers are all adults who have made the choice to play these sports despite the dangers. Minors need parental **permission** to play these sports as well. Safety is also a high **priority** with violent sports. These sports have rules against **excessive** violence. Special equipment keeps the athletes safe. For instance, football players wear helmets and lots of padding to prevent injury. When there is an injury, medical professionals are always nearby to treat the athletes. A final point to consider is that millions of people watch these sports to relax and to have fun. Prohibiting them would only make these people very unhappy.

Vocabulary Check

Choose the correct word for each definition.

> compelling   imitate   permission   priority   excessive

1 to do the same thing as someone _____
2 the right to do something given by a person in power _____
3 something that is more important than others so must be done first _____
4 causing someone to believe or agree _____
5 more than is needed; too much _____

Comprehension Questions

Check the correct answer for each question.

1 What is true about football, boxing, and wrestling?
  ☐ They are currently illegal to play.
  ☐ They cause injury and occasionally death.

2 Why does Muhammad Ali have trouble walking and talking?
  ☐ Because he suffered an accident while boxing
  ☐ Because he received lots of head injuries as a boxer

3 How would the rights of adults be affected by a ban on violent sports?
  ☐ They would not be allowed the freedom to play the sports they want.
  ☐ They would need to get parental permission to play these sports.

4 What are some safety measures taken for violent sports?
  ☐ The sports have rules to encourage excessive violence.
  ☐ The athletes wear special equipment and can receive medical treatment.

Questions for Debate

Think of and share ideas to explore the debatable issues in the article. Be sure to state your opinion clearly and to provide one supporting idea for each opinion.

1 Do you enjoy watching violent sports such as boxing? Why or why not?

In my case, I _____

_____.

The reason I feel this way is _____

_____.

2 What are some other dangerous activities that are banned? Why are they banned?

Some other activities are _____

_____.

They are banned because _____

_____.

3 Is it possible to stop everybody from playing violent sports? Why or why not?

I believe that _____

_____.

For example, _____

_____.

4 What are some feasible alternatives to a complete ban on violent sports?

One alternative is _____

_____.

This would be beneficial because _____

_____.

5 How could a ban on violent sports affect other social freedoms?

It is my firm conviction that _____

_____.

For instance, _____

_____.

Opinion Examples

Look at the opinion examples about the motion below and answer the questions.

Motion: Violent sports should not be legal to play.

Opinion A Track 02

Boxing is not a sport; it is legalized assault. That's why I believe it and other violent sports should be banned. Just look at how short the careers of these athletes are. Few professional football players complete more than four seasons. Some boxers quit after just one match. Simply put, violent sports can easily destroy a person's body. Allowing these brutal sports to be played also sends the message that violence is acceptable and even fun. Rather than encouraging violence, we should promote teamwork and safety. Banning violent sports will not end violence altogether, but it will play a role in making the world more peaceful.

Opinion B Track 03

Our world today is filled with too many laws. People need more freedom, not less. This is why banning violent sports is a horrible idea. First of all, consider the loss of personal freedom. The adult athletes who play these sports make a calculated choice to do so. They know the dangers and accept them. Society should not prevent these people from playing the sports they love. Moreover, watching violent sports is thrilling. This is not a new concept. Think of the gladiators who fought to the death in ancient Rome. By comparison, the violent sports of today are tame. Let people have fun. Let them play and watch violent sports.

1. Underline the main idea of each opinion.

2. Which opinion is for the topic? Which one is against it?
   - FOR: _____
   - AGAINST: _____

3. What supporting ideas does each opinion give?
   - Opinion A: _____
   - Opinion B: _____

4. Create one more supporting idea for each argument.
   - Opinion A: _____
   - Opinion B: _____

Skills for Debate

Read and learn how to create expert opinion examples.

How Can You Create Expert Opinion Examples?

Expert opinion examples use ideas and information generated by experts from many different subjects. You can find expert opinions on **the Internet** and in **newspapers**, **magazines**, and **books**. Look for **keywords** that explain **why your argument is correct**. Give between one and four sentences that prove your team's point. When giving your expert opinion, start it with **introductory phrases**. These include "According to (expert's name and job title)," "Our argument is clearly supported by the opinion of (expert's name and job title)," and "(Expert's name and job title) strongly believes that."

Practicing Debate Skills

Create examples for each argument by using the expert opinions. First, choose the part you want to introduce with a phrase and then draw parallels to the arguments.

1 Violent sports present too many health risks for them to be legal.

Expert Opinion – Dr. Patricia Wood, medical doctor
The number of injuries associated with violent sports is excessively high. Sports such as football often result in cuts, bruises, torn ligaments, and broken bones. Almost anyone who plays these violent sports suffers at least one serious injury during their careers. Boxers are especially likely to get hurt and to suffer severe head injuries. This can affect their speaking ability and motor skills for the rest of their lives.

Example: _____

_____

2 Banning violent sports is a denial of personal freedoms.

Expert Opinion – Sean Levy, lawyer
One of the main freedoms our society gives is freedom of choice. People should be allowed to do anything they want as long as it does not put anyone else at risk. However, a ban on violent sports takes away this right. Adults have the right to play violent sports if they want to. They know the risks yet choose to play. We should not sit back and let this right be taken away.

Example: _____

_____

Unit 01   B Debating the Topic

Creating Your Debate

Motion: Violent sports should not be legal to play.

What are your arguments? Get into two groups and plan for the debate. Decide whether your team is FOR (agree) or AGAINST (disagree) the motion. Then, create your ARE: Argument, Reason, and Example. Use the example arguments below and the research from your workbook to help create your arguments.

■ **Example Arguments**

FOR

Argument

Violent sports are simply too dangerous to play.

Reason

Most sports require players to score points while using equipment such as bats and balls. Violent sports are different in that they require players to win by attacking each other. This is an unnecessarily violent way for athletes to compete.

Example

Football, boxing, and wrestling have all had athletes die during matches as a result of injuries they received during play. One such athlete is South Korean boxer Yosam Choi. He died during a boxing match in 2008.

AGAINST

Argument

Many safety measures are taken to protect the athletes.

Reason

All sports have measures to make sure the players are safe. For one, the athletes wear protective gear. Medical staff are also on hand to treat the athletes. Finally, each sport has rules to prevent unnecessary violence.

Example

For instance, football players wear lots of padding and strong helmets to protect their bodies. There are also specific rules against hitting players who have already fallen on the ground.

■ Arguments FOR/AGAINST the Motion

ARGUMENT 1

Argument

_____
_____
_____
_____
_____
_____

Reason

_____
_____
_____
_____
_____

Example

_____
_____
_____
_____
_____
_____

ARGUMENT 2

Argument

_____
_____
_____
_____
_____
_____

Reason

_____
_____
_____
_____
_____

Example

_____
_____
_____
_____
_____
_____

ARGUMENT 3

Argument

_____
_____
_____
_____
_____
_____

Reason

_____
_____
_____
_____
_____

Example

_____
_____
_____
_____
_____
_____

Actual Debate

Now, it's time to debate. Use the flow chart below to help you organize the debate.
The introductory expressions have been provided to help you. Put your arguments in logical order and make clear rebuttals to the opposing team's arguments.

Agree Opening Statement
We strongly feel that _____
_____.

Agree Argument 1
The first point we would like to mention is ____
_____
_____
_____
_____.

Rebuttal 1
We must disagree with your argument since ____
_____
_____.

Agree Argument 2
As for our next point, _____
_____
_____.

Rebuttal 2
Despite the opposing team's argument that ____
_____,
we contend that _____
_____.

Agree Argument 3
The last point we will present is _____
_____
_____.

Agree Closing Statement
In conclusion, it is clear that _____
_____.

Disagree Opening Statement
Our side holds a different view. We believe that _____.

Rebuttal 1
Your assumption that _____
_____ is wrong because
_____.

Disagree Argument 1
The first reason we oppose this topic is _____
_____.

Rebuttal 2
Once again, our opponents are mistaken.
The fact is _____
_____.

Disagree Argument 2
Second of all, _____
_____.

Rebuttal 3
Your third argument overlooks the fact that ____
_____
_____.

Disagree Argument 3
We would like to conclude our arguments with _____
_____.

Disagree Closing Statement
To summarize, our view of this topic is _____
_____.

Sum Up the Debate

Finish the debate summary.

AGREEING SIDE'S ARGUMENT

The issue of this debate was _____.

The first team favored the topic by claiming that _____.

They started off by mentioning that _____.

Their evidence was _____
_____.

Next, they argued that _____.

The supporting details they gave were _____
_____.

For their final point, they explained that _____.

Specifically, they talked about _____
_____.

DISAGREEING SIDE'S ARGUMENT

The second team contended that _____
_____.

The first argument they made was _____.

They justified this by mentioning that _____
_____.

The team also felt that _____.

Their example was _____
_____.

Finally, they affirmed that _____.

To go into detail, they mentioned that _____
_____.

Unit 02
Part-Time Jobs for Teenagers

A. Discuss the following questions as a class.
1. What do you see in the picture above?
2. How many hours per week do you think the girl in the picture works?
3. What do you think the girl can learn by having a part-time job?

B. Answer the following questions with a partner.
1. Have you ever been paid to do any work? If so, what work did you do, and how much did you earn?
2. When do you think a person is old enough to have a part-time job?
3. What problems can occur if teenagers work part time while going to school?

Unit 02 A Learning about the Topic

Should teenagers be allowed to work at part-time jobs?

Read the passage and underline the main ideas.  Track 04

Around 80 percent of American teenagers have at least one part-time job during high school. Most of these teens work during the summer, but some of them choose to work throughout the year. A number of parents, teachers, and lawmakers believe that teenagers are too young to work and attend school at the same time. Even so, there are several **persuasive** reasons that these young people should be allowed to keep their part-time jobs.

For one, teenagers can learn **marketable** skills by working at a part-time job. They learn job skills such as being on time for work, following directions, and working efficiently. Part-time jobs teach students how to manage their money and to develop good spending habits. At the same time, having a part-time job rarely affects teenagers' academic work. Many countries limit the number of hours teenagers may work. For instance, teenagers in the United States can only work a **maximum** of 20 hours a week. This gives them enough time to study and to do well at school. We must also keep in mind that teenagers can be more independent when they work at a part-time job. They can go out and socialize with their friends without having to ask their parents for money. This helps young people become more mature and responsible.

While a lot of teenagers want to have part-time jobs, not everybody believes they should have them. One worry is that teenagers are too irresponsible to have jobs. Some employers complain that teenagers are not mature enough to do their jobs properly. Teens are more likely to show up late for work or to skip it completely and to make mistakes at the job. Likewise, teenagers are less likely to listen to directions or to follow their manager's **feedback**. Additionally, there are academic concerns. Many part-time jobs have students work on weekday evenings after school. Their work hours drastically cut into a student's study time. It is, therefore, not surprising that students who work tend to have lower grades than nonworking students. Working teenagers can also use their money and get into trouble by doing harmful activities, such as **underage** drinking.

Vocabulary Check

Choose the correct word for each definition.

| persuasive | marketable | maximum | feedback | underage |

1 helpful information that helps someone do better _____
2 the most or highest amount _____
3 able to cause people to do or believe something _____
4 too young to do something legally _____
5 able to be sold; wanted by buyers or employers _____

Comprehension Questions

Check the correct answer for each question.

1 Why do some people believe teenagers should not have part-time jobs?
  - ☐ Because they might cause problems at work
  - ☐ Because they are too young to work and study

2 What are some skills that teenagers can learn by working at part-time jobs?
  - ☐ They can learn how to follow orders and to develop good money management skills.
  - ☐ They can learn how to respond to customers' directions and to save money.

3 What are some complaints managers have about working teenagers?
  - ☐ Teenage employees may not be on time for work and make more errors.
  - ☐ Teenage employees may not understand how to do their jobs properly.

4 When do students usually have to work at their part-time jobs?
  - ☐ On weekends
  - ☐ On weekday evenings

Questions for Debate

Think of and share ideas to explore the debatable issues in the article. Be sure to state your opinion clearly and to provide one supporting idea for each opinion.

1 At what age do you believe that a teenager is ready to work at a part-time job?

My belief is _____

_____.

I feel this way since _____

_____.

2 What are some reasons that teenagers work at part-time jobs?

Some of the reasons are _____

_____.

To go into more detail, _____

_____.

3 How can working at a part-time job affect a student's ability to study?

From my perspective, it appears that _____

_____.

For example, _____

_____.

4 Should governments create laws limiting the number of hours teenagers can work? Why or why not?

My opinion is that _____

_____.

More specifically, _____

_____.

5 Which is more important: getting work experience as a teenager or studying hard at school?

I contend that _____

_____.

The reason I believe this is _____

_____.

Opinion Examples

Look at the opinion examples about the motion below and answer the questions.

Motion: Teenagers should be allowed to work at part-time jobs.

Opinion A Track 05

As teenagers, my parents both had part-time jobs. Neither of them ever said they regretted working. This is why I believe teens should be permitted to work. One reason is that they can develop useful skills. Most teenagers are used to dealing with their parents and teachers. Working is different. The managers expect them to do a good job all of the time; otherwise, they will get fired. This teaches teenagers the value of hard work. Just as importantly, working part-time gives teenagers more independence. Even though most jobs for teens don't pay much money, it is enough money for them to rely less on their parents and to be more independent.

Opinion B Track 06

Getting real world experience is important, but I think it is better to learn this lesson later in life. When teenagers work, they often face poor conditions. They do physically demanding jobs such as waiter or fast-food cook. These jobs are tiring and sometimes dangerous. Managers may not treat teens well because they are young and naive. For many teens, working is an unpleasant experience. Moreover, most part-time jobs pay little money—only about minimum wage. It is much better to study hard in school and become qualified for higher-paying jobs as adults than to work at a fast-food restaurant making $8 an hour.

1. Underline the main idea of each opinion.

2. Which opinion is for the topic? Which one is against it?
   - FOR: _____
   - AGAINST: _____

3. What supporting ideas does each opinion give?
   - Opinion A: _____
   - Opinion B: _____

4. Create one more supporting idea for each argument.
   - Opinion A: _____
   - Opinion B: _____

Skills for Debate

Read and learn how to create expert opinion examples.

How Can You Create Expert Opinion Examples?

Using expert opinions effectively requires you to **draw parallels** between the opinion and your argument. After you explain the key words from your expert opinion, you need **show** clearly how the **opinion relates to your argument**. Start by using the phrases "This relates to our point because," "This finding clearly proves our situation since," and "To make this point clear, consider that…." Go on to **explain the similarities** between the expert opinion and your argument. Describe a **process** that proves your argument. You can also mention a **result** that proves your argument.

Practicing Debate Skills

Create examples for each argument by using the expert opinions. Choose the part you want to introduce with a phrase and then draw parallels to the arguments.

1 Teenagers who have part-time jobs usually do worse in school.

> **Expert Opinion - Frank Gray, high school math teacher**
>
> I've been a high school teacher for close to 20 years. In that time, I've taught plenty of students who decided to make some money at part-time jobs after school. Almost all of these students end up getting worse grades because of their jobs. And each year, there seems to be at least one student who ends up quitting school all because of a part-time job. It's a shame to see this happen to good students.

Example: _The opinion of_ _____.

Parallel: _This relates to our point because_ _____.

2 Having part-time jobs teaches teenagers to be more responsible.

> **Expert Opinion – Maria Hernandez, grocery store assistant manager**
>
> About half of our front-end staff members are teenagers working part time. A lot of them are immature at first. Over time, though, you start to see these teens finish their work quickly and make their customers happy. The teens know that they can get pay raises by doing quality work, so that also motivates them. Really, you'd be surprised how dedicated and hardworking teenagers can become by working part time at our store.

Example: _Allow us to mention the experience of_ _____.

Parallel: _To make this point clear, consider that_ _____.

Unit 02 B Debating the Topic

Creating Your Debate

Motion: Teenagers should be allowed to work at part-time jobs.

What are your arguments? Get into two groups and plan for the debate. Decide whether your team is FOR (agree) or AGAINST (disagree) the motion. Then, create your ARE: Argument, Reason, and Example. Use the example arguments below and the research from your workbook to help create your arguments.

■ **Example Arguments**

FOR

Argument

Working at part-time jobs gives teenagers real world experience.

Reason

Having a job is different from going to school. Managers have specific expectations from their employees. They will not tolerate an employee who does not do his or her work or who always shows up late. Teenagers must become more responsible and mature when they work at a job.

Example

At my first part-time job, my manager would always severely criticize me whenever I made a mistake. At first, this made me feel discouraged, but I eventually learned to do my job better and to make fewer mistakes.

AGAINST

Argument

The main responsibility of teenagers is studying, not working.

Reason

During our teenage years, our priority is to get good grades in school. The main factor for being successful later in life is being a good student. However, the skills we learn at a part-time job do little to prepare us for a better future.

Example

Researchers found that students who spend more time working as teenagers tend to earn less money as adults. The researchers concluded that these teens did worse in school, were less likely to go to college, and got lower-paying jobs later on.

■ Arguments FOR/AGAINST the Motion

ARGUMENT 1

Argument

_____
_____
_____
_____
_____
_____

Reason

_____
_____
_____
_____
_____

Example

_____
_____
_____
_____
_____
_____

ARGUMENT 2

Argument

_____
_____
_____
_____
_____
_____

Reason

_____
_____
_____
_____
_____

Example

_____
_____
_____
_____
_____
_____

ARGUMENT 3

Argument

_____
_____
_____
_____
_____
_____

Reason

_____
_____
_____
_____
_____

Example

_____
_____
_____
_____
_____
_____

Actual Debate

Now, it's time to debate. Use the flow chart below to help you organize the debate.
The introductory expressions have been provided to help you. Put your arguments in logical order and make clear rebuttals to the opposing team's arguments.

Agree Opening Statement
It is our team's firm conviction that _____
_____
_____.

Agree Argument 1
The first point we want to mention is _____
_____
_____
_____.

Rebuttal 1
The con team mistakenly believes that _____
_____.
Instead, consider that _____
_____.

Agree Argument 2
We also support this motion since _____
_____
_____.

Rebuttal 2
Your argument is wrong because _____
_____
_____.

Agree Argument 3
For our final argument, let us point out that _____
_____.

Agree Closing Statement
It is our central argument that _____
_____
_____.

Disagree Opening Statement
As for our team, we are positive that _____
_____
_____.

Rebuttal 1
Your argument that _____
_____ does not make sense.
The fact is _____
_____.

Disagree Argument 1
To share our first argument, consider that _____
_____.

Rebuttal 2
We disagree once again. Our opinion is _____
_____.

Disagree Argument 2
Our second supporting argument is _____
_____.

Rebuttal 3
You said that _____
_____. However, we have to point out that _____
_____.

Disagree Argument 3
For our last point, consider that _____
_____.

Disagree Closing Statement
Our overall opinion about this topic is _____
_____.

Sum Up the Debate

Finish the debate summary.

AGREEING SIDE'S ARGUMENT

The topic of today's debate was _____.

The pro team defended that notion that _____.

Their opening argument was _____.

This was supported by their example of _____
_____.

Second of all, they presented the idea that _____.

To go into further detail, they explained that _____
_____.

Their final reason was _____.

For instance, _____
_____.

DISAGREEING SIDE'S ARGUMENT

The other team attacked the motion by claiming that _____
_____.

For one, they felt that _____.

For instance, _____
_____.

The next point they brought up was _____.

In particular, they mentioned _____
_____.

As for their concluding argument, they stated that _____.

They elaborated upon this by highlighting that _____
_____.

Chapter 2

Creating Statistical Examples

Unit 03 Teaching Practical Subjects

Unit 04 Child Curfews

Unit 03: Teaching Practical Subjects

WARM-UP

A. Discuss the following questions as a class.

1. What do you see in the picture above?
2. How often do you think people use this type of math after finishing school?
3. Are there other types of math that are more useful in people's daily lives?

B. Answer the following questions with a partner.

1. What are three skills that you think are very helpful in people's daily lives?
2. Do many schools teach these skills to their students? Why or why not?
3. What are some drawbacks of teaching students practical skills?

Should students learn more practical subjects at school?

Read the passage and underline the main ideas.  Track 07

By the time most students finish high school, they will be able to read complex novels, do advanced algebra, and write argumentative essays. In comparison, only a few students will know how to read a job contract, calculate **interest** from savings accounts, or write a **résumé**. All of these are examples of practical skills that are necessary in people's daily lives. As important as having practical skills is, few schools teach them. Perhaps they should.

First of all, practical skills are the ones that people use and directly benefit from throughout their lives. As adults, students will always need to know how to **negotiate** the conditions of a job. They must learn how to earn more interest from savings accounts. Conversely, knowing how to do geometry or to write poetry is less useful. Beyond being useful, practical skills can help students be more interested in their studies. Some students may question the benefit of learning school subjects with little real-world use. With practical studies, students will clearly see the benefits of learning them. The most important reason is that people hardly ever have the chance to learn practical skills. It is true that some people can become better at negotiating contracts or investing money over time. There are others, though, who will never learn these practical skills. This is why schools must teach these subjects.

It is unlikely, though, that schools will stop focusing on academic education. The subjects that students learn at school are often complex and **abstract**. Most students can only learn these complicated ideas with the help of a good teacher and an organized curriculum. Practical skills are much easier to learn alone by comparison. Academic skills also develop students' minds. They can become more critical thinkers who are knowledgeable about the world by studying academic subjects at school. Subjects such as algebra may not directly be **pertinent** for our daily lives. However, the mental abilities students develop by studying it can improve their lives. Finally, it is easier for schools to evaluate students based on their academic skills. They can easily determine which students are the most intelligent and hardworking.

Vocabulary Check

Choose the correct word for each definition.

interest	résumé	negotiate	abstract	pertinent

1 to agree about something by formally discussing it _____

2 money paid by a bank for keeping money in a savings account _____

3 a document that lists your work experience and education _____

4 related to the thing being thought or discussed _____

5 relating to ideas and concepts rather than people or objects _____

Comprehension Questions

Check the correct answer for each question.

1 What is considered to be a practical skill? Choose TWO correct answers.
- ☐ doing advanced algebra
- ☐ calculating savings account interest
- ☐ reading job contracts
- ☐ writing argumentative essays

2 How can teaching practical subjects make students more interested in their studies?
- ☐ Because they will understand the real-world benefit of them
- ☐ Because they will need the help of a good teacher and curriculum

3 In what way can studying algebra have practical benefits?
- ☐ It helps students learn math skills used in daily life.
- ☐ It helps students develop their critical-thinking skills.

4 What can schools find out from teaching academic subjects?
- ☐ They can see which students are smart and hardworking.
- ☐ They can determine which students will earn the most money.

Questions for Debate

Think of and share ideas to explore the debatable issues in the article. Be sure to state your opinion clearly and to provide one supporting idea for each opinion.

1 Which subjects that you learn at school do you think are important for your future?

Some of the subjects include _____

_____.

To be more specific, _____

_____.

2 Why do you think schools mainly focus on teaching academic subjects?

It is my feeling that _____

_____.

What I mean by this is _____

_____.

3 Can it be useful to study subjects that do not apply to real-world situations? Explain.

To me, it is clear that _____

_____.

For instance, _____

_____.

4 In what ways can learning practical skills contribute to a person's success?

I think that _____

_____.

In order to explain further, let me point out that _____

_____.

5 Do you think more schools will teach practical skills in the future? Why or why not?

I anticipate that _____

_____.

The reason for this is _____

_____.

Opinion Examples

Look at the opinion examples about the motion below and answer the questions.

Motion: Students would benefit greatly from learning practical subjects in school.

Opinion A Track 08

I completely agree that people should learn practical skills. But they should do this after they get their academic education. School has always been a place to learn about deep knowledge. This is why schools teach world history, algebra, and Shakespeare. Schools teach these subjects not because they are practical, but because they are part of our culture. Learning this information can deeply shape a person and his or her view of the world. Besides, academic knowledge still has practical uses. It develops our critical-thinking skills. It gives us knowledge to do work that contributes to society. In short, we need academic knowledge to make our world a better place.

Opinion B Track 09

I'm always surprised when I hear about highly educated people who don't have any idea about saving their money or fixing the kitchen sink. This shows why we need practical education at schools. One reason is that practical skills are the ones which directly improve our lives. We need to know how to find jobs, build our savings, and deal with housing and car issues in our lives. Few people learn these skills until they are older, if ever. At the same time, many of the subjects we learn at school are not useful. Literature, art, and geometry are interesting, but we rarely need this knowledge in our daily lives.

1. Underline the main idea of each opinion.

2. Which opinion is for the topic? Which one is against it?
   - FOR: _____
   - AGAINST: _____

3. What supporting ideas does each opinion give?
   - Opinion A: _____
   - Opinion B: _____

4. Create one more supporting idea for each argument.
   - Opinion A: _____
   - Opinion B: _____

Skills for Debate

Read and learn how to create statistical examples.

How Can You Create Statistical Examples?

Statistics are information given through **numbers**. They **explain measurements** about a variety of factors, such as grade point averages, average salaries, and life expectancies. The first step in using statistics is **finding your data**. Choose information which clearly **supports your argument**. To use your statistic, you must **summarize what it means**. Explain what the statistic is about, such as which group of people it covers. Then give **one or two points of data** that prove your point.

Practicing Debate Skills

Read the following argument and statistics. Use the information to create a statistical example. Define the statistic and explain the important data. Some words have been provided to help you.

Argument: Students who study practical subjects in school are more likely to be successful as adults.

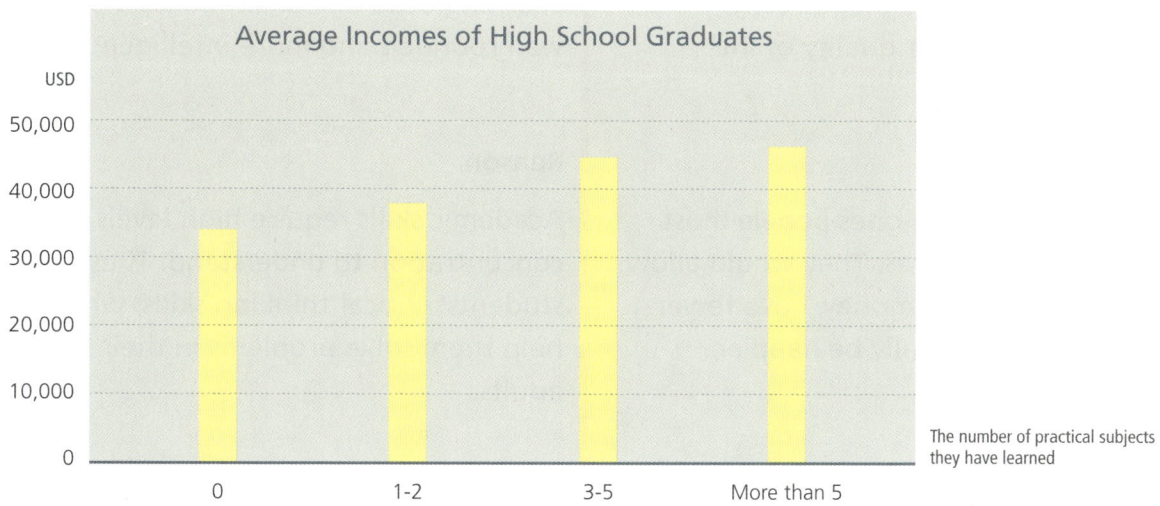

Example: *One statistic found that* _____

The specific findings were _____

Unit 03 B Debating the Topic

Creating Your Debate

Motion: Students would benefit greatly from learning practical subjects at school.

What are your arguments? Get into two groups and plan for the debate. Decide whether your team is FOR (agree) or AGAINST (disagree) the motion. Then, create your ARE: Argument, Reason, and Example. Use the example arguments below and the research from your workbook to help create your arguments.

■ Example Arguments

FOR

Argument

Students can get skills that directly contribute to a better quality of life.

Reason

Practical skills are the ones people must have to live better lives. They would allow people to save more money, have fewer problems, and generally be happier.

Example

Few people know how to save and invest their money properly. When they get older, they need to work past retirement age because they did not set aside enough money.

AGAINST

Argument

Learning academic skills makes a person well rounded and more intelligent.

Reason

Academic skills require high levels of concentration to understand. They develop students' critical-thinking skills, which will help them solve problems in their lives as adults.

Example

Studying literature helps students critically analyze situations. This enables them to understand problems from various angles and could help them find better solutions.

Arguments FOR/AGAINST the Motion

ARGUMENT 1	ARGUMENT 2	ARGUMENT 3
Argument	**Argument**	**Argument**
Reason	**Reason**	**Reason**
Example	**Example**	**Example**

Actual Debate

Now, it's time to debate. Use the flow chart below to help you organize the debate.
The introductory expressions have been provided to help you. Put your arguments in logical order and make clear rebuttals to the opposing team's arguments.

Agree Opening Statement
Our opinion is that _____
_____ is advantageous.

Disagree Opening Statement
In contrast, we believe that _____
_____.

Agree Argument 1
To begin with, we argue that _____
_____
_____
_____.

Rebuttal 1
Despite the opposition's belief that _____
_____, the truth remains that
_____
_____.

Disagree Argument 1
To share our first argument, consider that
_____
_____.

Rebuttal 1
Your team claims that _____
_____,
but we believe that _____
_____.

Rebuttal 2
Your statement that _____
_____
does not hold water because _____
_____.

Agree Argument 2
The next important factor to consider is that
_____
_____.

Disagree Argument 2
We must also point out that _____
_____.

Rebuttal 2
While the opposite team believes that _____
_____,
it is worth mentioning that _____
_____.

Rebuttal 3
The opposing team's argument is flawed due to the fact that _____
_____.

Agree Argument 3
Our final argument is _____
_____.

Disagree Argument 3
Our third and final point is _____
_____.

Agree Closing Statement
Despite our opponent's claims, we maintain that _____.

Disagree Closing Statement
Our team still feels that _____
_____.

Sum Up the Debate

Finish the debate summary.

AGREEING SIDE'S ARGUMENT

This debate topic focused on _____.

The agree team's central idea was _____.

They started off by arguing that _____.

Their example was _____
_____.

Second, they explained that _____.

Their supporting detail was _____
_____.

Their third argument was _____.

For instance, _____
_____.

DISAGREEING SIDE'S ARGUMENT

The opposing team attacked the topic and claimed that _____
_____.

First, they argued that _____.

They specifically mentioned that _____
_____.

Their next point was _____.

For example, _____
_____.

Their final argument was _____.

The detail they shared was _____
_____.

Unit 04 Child Curfews

WARM-UP

A. Discuss the following questions as a class.
1. What do you see in the picture above?
2. Why do you think the officer is talking to the girl?
3. What are some possible problems of enforcing child curfews?

B. Answer the following questions with a partner.
1. How late do you usually stay out without your parents?
2. Do you think child curfews can help prevent crimes? Why or why not?
3. What are ways in which child curfews can be inconvenient for children?

Unit 04 A Learning about the Topic

Should governments make curfew laws for children?

Read the passage and underline the main ideas. Track 10

The world can be a dangerous place for children, especially at night. Nighttime is when children are most likely to be attacked, kidnapped, and even murdered. To help keep children safe, some city and national governments have **proposed** children's curfews. These are laws that make it illegal for children to be outside the home during certain hours, usually from about 10 PM to 6 AM. But are child curfews really effective? Are they worth having in spite of the loss of personal freedoms they impose?

One shortcoming of child curfews is that they are too **restrictive**. In most cases, children are perfectly safe being out during evenings. They may simply be playing or hanging out with friends. Child curfew laws unfairly control the lives of children who are innocently having fun. Furthermore, there is no **guarantee** that forcing children to be at home will keep them safe. Children can still face problems at home, such as fighting with siblings. Other children must deal with abusive parents. In these instances, child curfews do little to keep children safe. Moreover, enforcing child curfews can be an unnecessary burden on police forces. Rather than catching serious criminals, the police would have to spend lots of time enforcing the child curfews. This is a waste of police resources.

There are still many advantages of child curfews despite the drawbacks. As already mentioned, the nighttime is when children face the most danger outside. The number of dangerous people on the streets rises sharply after sunset. Children are young and vulnerable, making them easy targets for criminals. By **enacting** child curfews, children will be forced to stay safely at home. Likewise, there is very much evidence to suggest that young people are actually responsible for crime. In some large cities in America and Europe, a number of teenagers are part of youth **gangs**. They attack and rob citizens at night. Child curfews can stop these teenagers from breaking the law. Families can also benefit from curfews. Parents would need to spend more time taking care of their children. As a result, families would have deeper ties. This would create stronger communities as a whole.

Vocabulary Check

Choose the correct word for each definition.

| propose | restrictive | guarantee | enact | gang |

1 to make something into a law _____
2 to suggest a plan for others to consider _____
3 a promise that something will happen _____
4 a group of criminals _____
5 limiting or controlling something _____

Comprehension Questions

Check the correct answer for each question.

1 What is the main reason governments want to create child curfews?
 - ☐ To make it illegal for children to be outside at night
 - ☐ To keep children safe from danger at night

2 Why might child curfews do little to keep children safe? Choose TWO correct answers.
 - ☐ They might fight with their brothers and sisters.
 - ☐ They might be abused by their parents.
 - ☐ They could be hanging out with their friends.
 - ☐ They might be having innocent fun.

3 How can child curfews waste police resources?
 - ☐ Because police officers would have to keep the children safe
 - ☐ Because police officers would not have time to catch serious criminals

4 What advantages do child curfews have for families?
 - ☐ They would help parents build stronger relationships with their children.
 - ☐ They would teach parents better ways to take care of their children.

Questions for Debate

Think of and share ideas to explore the debatable issues in the article. Be sure to state your opinion clearly and to provide one supporting idea for each opinion.

1 What are some dangers that children face by being out at night?

Some of the dangers are _____
_____.

For example, _____
_____.

2 Would child curfews mainly benefit or harm families? Explain.

It is my feeling that _____
_____.

I feel this way because _____
_____.

3 Would you want your community to adopt a child curfew law? Why or why not?

My opinion is _____
_____.

To be more specific, _____
_____.

4 Do you think it is right for the government to restrict personal freedoms by making child curfews? Why or why not?

To me, it seems that _____
_____.

For instance, _____
_____.

5 Instead of creating child curfew laws, what are other ways to keep communities safe at night?

I think it would be better to _____
_____.

More specifically, _____
_____.

Opinion Examples

Look at the opinion examples about the motion below and answer the questions.

Motion: Child curfews are ineffective and should not be adopted.

Opinion A Track 11

My city has child curfews, and I'm happy about that. They have done a lot to keep young people safer. I know that my neighborhood is a bit scary at night. There are dangerous people out who can hurt children. Before the curfew, kids were sometimes attacked and kidnapped at night, but now that doesn't happen. In addition to safety, child curfews help families. The curfews allow families to spend more time together. This can help them develop better relationships. In my case, my father and I have gotten to know each other better because of the curfews. We now spend lots more time talking to each other because I have to be at home.

Opinion B Track 12

Everybody can agree that we should keep children safe. Unfortunately, child curfews are not part of the solution. The idea behind curfews for young people is that they would be safer at home. We all know that this isn't always the case. A number of children are abused at home. For them, being on the streets is safer. In any case, there are many legitimate reasons children would be out at night. These include running errands and coming home from studying. Making child curfews would place an unnecessary burden on these children. If governments are serious about keeping children safe, they need to keep more criminals off the streets and protect abused children.

1 Underline the main idea of each opinion.

2 Which opinion is for the topic? Which one is against it?
   • FOR: _____
   • AGAINST: _____

3 What supporting ideas does each opinion give?
   • Opinion A: _____
   • Opinion B: _____

4 Create one more supporting idea for each argument.
   • Opinion A: _____
   • Opinion B: _____

Skills for Debate

Read and learn how to create statistical examples.

How Can You Create Statistical Examples?

After you define your statistics and give the data, it is necessary to explain **how they are related to your argument**. Mention the information **to prove your point** or **to disprove the opposite team's arguments**. Following this, draw conclusions that show why your arguments are correct. Use phrases such as "This statistic indicates that," "As proven by this data," and "We can clearly see from this information that" to introduce this information.

Practicing Debate Skills

Read the following argument and statistics. Use the information to create a statistical example. Define the statistic and explain the important data. Then, make a conclusion about the statistics. Some words have been provided to help you.

Argument: Most child curfews are ineffective at reducing youth crime rates.

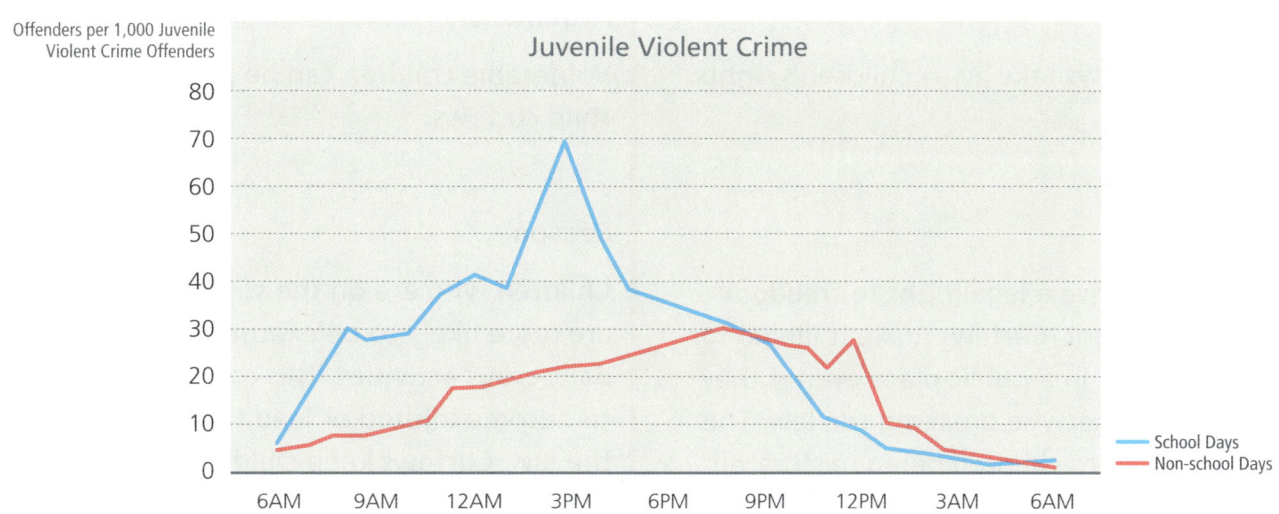

Example: *According to one statistic,* _____

_____.

The specific findings were _____

_____.

We can clearly see from this information that _____

_____.

49

Unit 04 B Debating the Topic

Creating Your Debate

Motion: Child curfews are ineffective and should not be adopted.

What are your arguments? Get into two groups and plan for the debate. Decide whether your team is FOR (agree) or AGAINST (disagree) the motion. Then, create your ARE: Argument, Reason, and Example. Use the example arguments below and the research from your workbook to help create your arguments.

■ **Example Arguments**

FOR

Argument

Child curfews take away children's rights.

Reason

Children have a legal right to freedom of movement. Curfews make it illegal for them to be in a public place even if they are not otherwise breaking the law. This could lead to children being mistreated simply because of their age.

Example

In the United States, the 1976 case *Missouri v. Danforth* stated that all citizens—even children—have a right to freedom of movement.

AGAINST

Argument

Vulnerable children can be protected by child curfews.

Reason

Children who are on the streets at night are more likely to be exposed to harmful or dangerous activities. This could cause them to become injured or lead them to break the law. Curfews keep children safe by preventing them from experiencing these harmful situations.

Example

Many large cities in the United States have adopted child curfews in an attempt to reduce teenage gang activity.

Arguments FOR/AGAINST the Motion

ARGUMENT 1	ARGUMENT 2	ARGUMENT 3
Argument	**Argument**	**Argument**
Reason	**Reason**	**Reason**
Example	**Example**	**Example**

Actual Debate

Now, it's time to debate. Use the flow chart below to help you organize the debate.
The introductory expressions have been provided to help you. Put your arguments in logical order and make clear rebuttals to the opposing team's arguments.

Agree Opening Statement
It is our conviction that _____.

Disagree Opening Statement
Contrarily, our team contends that _____.

Agree Argument 1
Our opening argument is _____.

Rebuttal 1
It is incorrect to assume that _____ due to the fact that _____.

Disagree Argument 1
To share our first idea, _____.

Rebuttal 1
Your argument is flawed considering that _____.

Rebuttal 2
We will refute this idea by stating that _____.

Agree Argument 2
We also support this motion because _____.

Disagree Argument 2
The next argument we would like to make is _____.

Rebuttal 2
Our opponents mistakenly believe that _____.

Rebuttal 3
Your argument overlooks the fact that _____.

Agree Argument 3
The final argument we will make is _____.

Disagree Argument 3
The last point we want to present is _____.

Agree Closing Statement
To summarize, _____.

Disagree Closing Statement
Our overall opinion is that _____.

Sum Up the Debate

Finish the debate summary.

AGREEING SIDE'S ARGUMENT

Today's debate topic was _____.

To support this motion, the first team argued that _____.

First of all, they posited that _____.

They proved this point by mentioning that _____
_____.

Their next argument was _____.

To be specific, _____
_____.

Lastly, the agree side claimed that _____.

Their example was _____
_____.

DISAGREEING SIDE'S ARGUMENT

On the other hand, the disagree team felt that _____
_____.

Their first claim was _____.

They mentioned _____
_____ to support their argument.

The next idea they brought up was that _____.

For instance, _____
_____.

Their closing argument was _____.

The supporting detail they gave was _____
_____.

53

Chapter 3

Creating Academic Studies Examples

Unit 05 Internet Censorship

Unit 06 Free Public Transportation

Unit 05 Internet Censorship

WARM-UP

A. Discuss the following questions as a class.
1. What do you see in the picture above?
2. How can Internet censorship affect freedom of speech?
3. Why is it important for citizens to have the right to share their ideas freely?

B. Answer the following questions with a partner.
1. What websites do you most often visit on the Internet?
2. Do you think any of the websites you enjoy should be censored?
3. How can Internet censorship protect the public?

Unit 05 A Learning about the Topic

Should governments be allowed to censor the Internet?

Read the passage and underline the main ideas. Track 13

Virtually all Internet search websites censor information. These websites intentionally **block** some of the information on the Internet. But in some cases, not only websites but also national governments choose to censor the Internet. These governments claim that this is for the good of the public. No doubt Internet censorship has its advantages. However, they may be **overshadowed** by its drawbacks.

The most obvious reason to censor the Internet is to restrict people from accessing harmful content. Millions of websites include material that many people would consider to be **immoral**. This would include websites that promote illegal activities, such as drug use and murder. Censoring the Internet stops people from viewing these sites and becoming ethically corrupt. Along the same reasoning, Internet censorship can prevent crime. The biggest crime online these days is illegal file sharing. People use peer-to-peer websites to steal music, television shows, and movies. Governments can block these sites by censoring the Internet. This would stop intellectual property theft. Another advantage of Internet censorship is that it can make people happier. People will be less likely to encounter depressing news or information through censorship. This would help them live more **carefree** lives.

A main criticism of Internet censorship is how it restricts people's freedom of choice. Internet censorship laws affect not only children but also adults. Adults are mature. They can view almost any content without serious **repercussions**. Therefore, they should be allowed to do what they want online as long as it does not hurt others. Another worry is that Internet censorship may prevent people from sharing their ideas freely. For instance, the Chinese government blocks social networking sites such as Facebook. They shut down blogs that criticize the government. While it is in the interest of the government to do so, the people are denied their right to free speech. Finally, Internet censorship could eventually lead governments to begin taking away other freedoms. Some worry that this will create a restrictive police-state environment.

Vocabulary Check

Choose the correct word for each definition.

block overshadow immoral carefree repercussion

1 to be in the way of something; to stop something   _____
2 to cause something to seem less important   _____
3 something bad that happens as a result of an action   _____
4 without worry or concern   _____
5 not morally good or right   _____

Comprehension Questions

Check the correct answer for each question.

1 Which of the following is true about censorship?
   ☐ Many websites that search the Internet use censorship for some information.
   ☐ National governments use censorship to hide information from the public.

2 How can accessing amoral content affect people?
   ☐ They might start using drugs or commit murder.
   ☐ They could become ethically corrupt.

3 In what way can governments stop intellectual property theft?
   ☐ They can sell people music, television shows, and movies.
   ☐ They can block peer-to-peer file-sharing websites.

4 Why do some people criticize the Chinese government's Internet censorship?
   ☐ Because it denies people their freedom of speech
   ☐ Because it has created a restrictive police state

Questions for Debate

Think of and share ideas to explore the debatable issues in the article. Be sure to state your opinion clearly and to provide one supporting idea for each opinion.

1 Who do you think benefits the most from Internet censorship? Explain.

To me, it seems that _____
_____.

I believe this since _____
_____.

2 Why do you think that governments try to censor the Internet?

They probably do this because _____
_____.

For example, _____
_____.

3 In your opinion, is it important for people to be able to share their ideas freely? Why or why not?

My opinion about this is _____
_____.

To be more specific, _____
_____.

4 Should people have the right to talk about illegal activities such as murder on the Internet?

It is my belief that _____
_____.

One point that illustrates this is _____
_____.

5 What are some repercussions that can occur if people do not have freedom of speech?

Some of the repercussions that can occur are _____
_____.

The problem with this is _____
_____.

Opinion Examples

Look at the opinion examples about the motion below and answer the questions.

Motion: Internet censorship is beneficial and will create a more stable society.

Opinion A Track 14

I strongly believe in freedom of speech. That is why I oppose all forms of censorship, including Internet censorship. Taking away people's freedom of speech can lead to more serious problems. For instance, people who cannot share their ideas are more likely to be controlled by their governments. They will live in fear of being arrested for sharing ideas that are against the law. In a free society, people should be allowed to say whatever they want. At the same time, Internet censorship denies people their freedom of choice. Adults should have the right to see whatever content they would like. It is not the government's decision to control what people can view and talk about online.

Opinion B Track 15

To me, we need Internet censorship to make society better. These days, there are numerous websites that allow people to break the law. Peer-to-peer websites are a strong example of this. Downloading movies and music is the same as stealing them, so it is completely right for the government to block these websites. Another benefit of censorship is that it can protect the most vulnerable members of society. Today's young people are exposed to harmful content such as violent games and videos through the Internet. Governments should block these types of materials online in order to prevent people from becoming amoral.

1. Underline the main idea of each opinion.

2. Which opinion is for the topic? Which one is against it?
   - FOR: _____
   - AGAINST: _____

3. What supporting ideas does each opinion give?
   - Opinion A: _____
   - Opinion B: _____

4. Create one more supporting idea for each argument.
   - Opinion A: _____
   - Opinion B: _____

Skills for Debate

Read and learn how to create academic studies examples.

How Can You Create Academic Studies Examples?

Academic studies are formal research conducted by universities, governments, and large research organizations. To use academic studies correctly, there are some points you must keep in mind. Start by explaining **who is responsible** for the study using phrases like "According to a study conducted by (researcher's or institution's name)." Second, mention **what the study is about**. The phrase "The primary focus of the study was…" makes the main goal of the study clear. Most importantly, describe **the findings of the study** with a phrase such as "What the researchers discovered was…"

Practicing Debate Skills

Read the following academic study article. Use the appropriate phrases and write who created the study, what the study focused on, and what the results were on the lines provided.

Academic Study

Professor Richard David at the University of Chicago recently conducted a study about the relationship between Internet censorship and happiness using the Internet. To conduct the study, David surveyed 1,200 citizens each in the United States and China. He asked them questions about how enjoyable their Internet experiences are. The professor hypothesized that more people in the United States would claim to be happier since the country has few censorship laws. Likewise, the lack of freedom online would reduce Chinese people's happiness. In the end, over two-thirds of Americans said that they are happy online. Surprisingly, a similar number of Chinese were happy with their Internet situation. Professor David believes that a minority of Americans do not like the inappropriate content online whereas many Chinese are happy since they are protected from it.

Phrases

The findings of the study were… / A study by… proves this. / To conduct the study, the professor…

_____

_____

_____

_____

Unit 05 B Debating the Topic

Creating Your Debate

Motion: Internet censorship is beneficial and will create a more stable society.

What are your arguments? Get into two groups and plan for the debate. Decide whether your team is FOR (agree) or AGAINST (disagree) the motion. Then, create your ARE: Argument, Reason, and Example. Use the example arguments below and the research from your workbook to help create your arguments.

■ Example Arguments

FOR

Argument

Internet censorship ensures that people will not be exposed to harmful content online.

Reason

Most websites online already block inappropriate content. However, there are some websites that focus exclusively on harmful and dangerous content. While a lot of these websites have warnings about the content, they are still easy for people to access. Thus, they should be censored.

Example

One study found that around 20 percent of websites have adult content. The governments in China and South Korea block these websites so that no one can access them.

AGAINST

Argument

Internet censorship denies people their freedom of choice.

Reason

Adult citizens have a right to decide for themselves what they should and should not see. If the government censors the Internet, they are not able to exercise this right.

Example

Almost all websites that have inappropriate and adult content have warnings. The people who access these sites do so by choice. If parents are concerned about their children, they can purchase software which censors the Internet.

Arguments FOR/AGAINST the Motion

ARGUMENT 1	ARGUMENT 2	ARGUMENT 3
Argument	**Argument**	**Argument**
Reason	**Reason**	**Reason**
Example	**Example**	**Example**

Actual Debate

Now, it's time to debate. Use the flow chart below to help you organize the debate.
The introductory expressions have been provided to help you. Put your arguments in logical order and make clear rebuttals to the opposing team's arguments.

Agree Opening Statement
Our side firmly believes that _____
_____
_____
_____ .

Disagree Opening Statement
We strongly oppose the notion that _____
_____
_____
_____ .

Agree Argument 1
The first argument we will make is _____
_____
_____
_____
_____ .

Rebuttal 1
To rebut this point, let us point out that _____
_____
_____ .

Disagree Argument 1
Our opening argument is _____
_____
_____ .

Rebuttal 1
We refute the idea that _____
_____
_____ .

Rebuttal 2
Your assumption is flawed because _____
_____
_____
_____ .

Agree Argument 2
Second of all, _____
_____
_____
_____ .

Disagree Argument 2
To add to our first point, _____
_____
_____
_____ .

Rebuttal 2
Once again, the con team has it wrong. In reality, _____
_____
_____ .

Rebuttal 3
In spite of your claim that _____
_____
we believe that _____
_____ .

Agree Argument 3
The final point we will mention is _____
_____
_____
_____ .

Disagree Argument 3
Our final argument is _____
_____
_____ .

Agree Closing Statement
For our closing statement, we feel that _____
_____
_____ .

Disagree Closing Statement
To summarize, we maintain that _____
_____
_____ .

Sum Up the Debate

Finish the debate summary.

AGREEING SIDE'S ARGUMENT

This debate topic focused on _____.

The overall belief of the agree team was _____.

For one, they claimed that _____.

To share their example, _____
_____.

Their second point was that _____.

In detail, they stated _____
_____.

The argument they shared last was _____.

For instance, _____
_____.

DISAGREEING SIDE'S ARGUMENT

The opposing team felt the opposite and claimed that _____
_____.

They began by arguing that _____.

To be specific, _____
_____.

The second argument they gave was that _____.

The notion that _____
_____ strengthened their claim.

Lastly, they said that _____.

Their supporting reasons were _____
_____.

65

Unit 06 Free Public Transportation

A. Discuss the following questions as a class.
1. What do you see in the picture above?
2. Why do you think some cities offer free public transportation?
3. How can making public transportation free improve people's lives?

B. Answer the following questions with a partner.
1. Which people do you think would get the most advantages from free public transportation?
2. How could making public transportation free affect the quality of service?
3. Where do you think the money to pay for public transportation comes from?

Unit 06 A Learning about the Topic

Should people not have to pay to use public transportation?

Read the passage and underline the main ideas. Track 16

Over 65 cities in 20 countries currently offer free public transportation. People in these cities can ride buses, trams, trains, and even ferries without having to pay a single **fare**. Most of these cities use tax money to cover the costs. It is clear that a large number of citizens can benefit from not having to pay for public transportation.

One of the strongest arguments in favor of no-charge public transportation is that it would improve people's lives. Without having to pay fares, people could use public transportation as much as they want. This would most notably help people with lower incomes, who often cannot afford to pay transportation fares. Making public transportation free would also improve traffic **congestion**. In cities such as Hasselt in Belgium, Ockelbo in Sweden, and Changning in China, free public transportation has greatly reduced road traffic. Having less congested roads make driving times much shorter while also cutting down on air pollution. Best of all, funding free public transportation would be simple. It would require only a **modest** increase in taxes. The tax increase could only be applied to people in higher income brackets. People with lower incomes, who benefit the most from free public transportation, would not need to pay.

All the same, free public transportation would require some major **tradeoffs**. Perhaps the most notable would be a decrease in the quality of service. So far, only small cities, where the number of riders is low, offer free public transportation. If large cities such as New York, London, or Seoul were to offer free public transportation, it could lead to huge crowds and poor service. This would likely **discourage** people from riding no-fare public transit. For many people, though, the most serious drawback would be paying more taxes. There is no promise that a tax increase would be small. Too much of a tax increase could present financial difficulties for a lot of people. Besides, some people do not ride public transportation. These people might resent having to pay taxes for a nonessential service that they never use.

Vocabulary Check

Choose the correct word for each definition.

| fare | congestion | modest | tradeoff | discourage |

1 to make people not want to do something _____
2 the money a person pays to travel on public transportation _____
3 something bad that comes along with something good _____
4 being full with too many things _____
5 not very large in size or amount _____

Comprehension Questions

Check the correct answer for each question.

1 How do most cities cover the costs of free public transportation?
   ☐ They charge higher fares.
   ☐ They use tax money.

2 Who would most clearly benefit from free public transportation?
   ☐ People who need to use public transportation very often
   ☐ People who do not make enough money to pay transportation fares

3 What happened in Belgium, Sweden, and China after introducing free public transportation?
   ☐ The roads became less congested, and the amount of air pollution was reduced.
   ☐ The buses and trains become too crowded, and the quality of service decreased.

4 How could free public transportation lead to public resentment?
   ☐ Because it would create financial difficulties for a number of people
   ☐ Because it would force people to pay for a service they do not use

Questions for Debate

Think of and share ideas to explorey the debatable issues in the article. Be sure to state your opinion clearly and to provide one supporting idea for each opinion.

1. How would people with lower incomes benefit from free public transportation?

   My feeling is that _____.

   This is due to the fact that _____.

2. Do you believe that larger cities such as New York and Seoul could have free public transportation? Why or why not?

   To me, it is obvious that _____.

   The reason is _____.

3. Should people be required to pay taxes on a service they do not use, such as public transportation?

   It is my contention that _____.

   For example, _____.

4. Is it as important to provide free public transportation as it is to provide health care or education? Explain.

   My opinion about the matter is _____.

   Think about how _____.

5. Rather than making public transportation free for everybody, what are other solutions that could be more financially beneficial?

   Some alternatives to fixing this problem include _____.

   These would be better because _____.

Opinion Examples

Look at the opinion examples about the motion below and answer the questions.

> **Motion: Public transportation should be free of charge for everybody.**

Opinion A Track 17

While I have no doubt that lots of people would love to have public transportation be free, I am not one of these people. Free public transportation would be beneficial, but it is not up to the government to provide it. The government should use tax money for essential services. These include health care, education, and trash collection. In comparison, free public transportation is not necessary. It would just present a burden for national governments. Rather than making public transportation free, I suggest having a system where people with low incomes pay lower fares. This way, they could afford to ride public busses and trains without having to raise taxes.

Opinion B Track 18

It is the responsibility of the government to provide services to the people. If the people want free public transportation, then the government must provide it. One reason is that it would help the less fortunate people in society. Millions of people all over the world can't afford to use public transportation. Getting rid of fares would help these people get to work and earn more money. Some people complain that taxes would have to go up. The good news is that the increase would probably be very small—just a few dollars more per year. People should be willing to pay a little more tax money for a service that benefits the greater society.

1 Underline the main idea of each opinion.

2 Which opinion is for the topic? Which one is against it?
- FOR: _____
- AGAINST: _____

3 What supporting ideas does each opinion give?
- Opinion A: _____
- Opinion B: _____

4 Create one more supporting idea for each argument.
- Opinion A: _____
- Opinion B: _____

Skills for Debate

Read and learn how to create academic studies examples.

How Can You Create Academic Studies Examples?

A common mistake students make when giving academic studies examples is not **explaining why the results are important**. After describing your study and giving the outcome, you should try to describe **why the results occurred** and **how the results prove your argument**. To do this, you must first focus on the **logic** of the study. Talk about the types of questions the researchers asked and how they got the answers. Afterward, **connect** the results to your argument and show how they prove your argument.

Practicing Debate Skills

Read the following argument and academic study below. Use the information to explain why the results occurred and how they relate to the argument. Some words have been provided to help you.

Argument

> Getting rid of fares on public transportation would save time and money.

Academic Study

> A group of engineers working for the New York Metropolitan Transit Authority calculated the amount of time and money spent to collect fares on public transportation. They determined that buses spent around 16 minutes per hour collecting fares. Such a long wait leads to longer travel times and less efficiency overall. The researchers also concluded that more than 6 percent of the MTA's budget is spent on collecting fares. This number includes the costs of maintaining ticket dispensing and collecting machines as well as wasted gas and electricity. Based on their findings, the engineers strongly suggest eliminating passenger fares altogether. The amount of time and money saved justifies the cost of providing free transportation services.

Example

A group of engineers working for New York's Metropolitan Transit Authority have determined that _____.

During the study, the researchers found that _____.

In the end, the researchers suggested that _____.

This example clearly proves our argument because _____.

Unit 06 B Debating the Topic

Creating Your Debate

Motion: Public transportation should be free of charge for everybody.

What are your arguments? Get into two groups and plan for the debate. Decide whether your team is FOR (agree) or AGAINST (disagree) the motion. Then, create your ARE: Argument, Reason, and Example. Use the example arguments below and the research from your workbook to help create your arguments.

- **Example Arguments**

FOR

Argument

Free public transportation would benefit a large number of people in our society.

Reason

Many of the people who ride public transportation have low incomes and have trouble paying current transportation fares. Free public transportation could be paid for by people with higher incomes. This would lead to greater equality.

Example

New York lawyer Ted Khee suggested that the city get rid of public transportation fares. He recommended that the city increase fares for driving across bridges and add congestion charges to make up for the lost income.

AGAINST

Argument

Free public transportation would disadvantage people who do not ride public transportation.

Reason

Many people resent having to pay more money in taxes and fees for a service they do not use. Instead of having all citizens pay to maintain free public transportation, it is better to have the riders simply pay fares.

Example

A recent poll of Americans found that 60 percent of respondents oppose making public transportation free. They feel that they should not have to pay for a service they do not use.

■ Arguments FOR/AGAINST the Motion

ARGUMENT 1

Argument

_____
_____
_____
_____
_____

Reason

_____
_____
_____
_____
_____

Example

_____
_____
_____
_____
_____

ARGUMENT 2

Argument

_____
_____
_____
_____
_____

Reason

_____
_____
_____
_____
_____

Example

_____
_____
_____
_____
_____

ARGUMENT 3

Argument

_____
_____
_____
_____
_____

Reason

_____
_____
_____
_____
_____

Example

_____
_____
_____
_____
_____

Actual Debate

Now, it's time to debate. Use the flow chart below to help you organize the debate.
The introductory expressions have been provided to help you. Put your arguments in logical order and make clear rebuttals to the opposing team's arguments.

Agree Opening Statement
We strongly believe that _____
_____
_____ .

Agree Argument 1
Our opening argument is _____
_____
_____
_____ .

Rebuttal 1
Unfortunately, your argument is flawed. _____
_____ .

Agree Argument 2
The next point we would like to mention is _____
_____ .

Rebuttal 2
Even though _____
_____ ,
we must point out that _____
_____ .

Agree Argument 3
Finally, _____
_____ .

Agree Closing Statement
We, the members of the pro team, feel that _____
_____
_____ .

Disagree Opening Statement
We feel that _____
_____ should be allowed.

Rebuttal 1
Your assumption that _____
_____ is wrong because
_____ .

Disagree Argument 1
The first reason we oppose this topic is _____
_____ .

Rebuttal 2
Our opponent's argument is flawed because
_____
_____
_____ .

Disagree Argument 2
Second of all, _____
_____ .

Rebuttal 3
Your third argument overlooks the fact that
_____
_____ .

Disagree Argument 3
We would like to conclude our arguments
with _____ .

Disagree Closing Statement
In conclusion, it is clear that _____
_____ .

Sum Up the Debate

Finish the debate summary.

AGREEING SIDE'S ARGUMENT

The topic of today's debate was _____.

The main opinion of the agreeing team was _____.

They started off by mentioning that _____.

Their evidence was _____
_____.

Second, they argued that _____.

For example, _____
_____.

For their final point, they explained that _____.

Specifically, they explained that _____
_____.

DISAGREEING SIDE'S ARGUMENT

The second team contended that _____
_____.

They began by stating that _____
_____.

For instance, _____
_____.

The team also felt that _____.

Their example was _____.

_____ was their final point.

In detail, they explained that _____
_____.

Chapter 4

Creating Effective Rebuttals

Unit 07 Punishing Parents

Unit 08 Studying Abroad

Unit 07 — Punishing Parents

WARM-UP

A. Discuss the following questions as a class.
1. What do you see in the picture above?
2. What do you think the girls are doing to the boy?
3. Who do you think should be responsible for the girls' actions?

B. Answer the following questions with a partner.
1. What does your school do to punish students who misbehave?
2. Do you think it is the parents' fault when their children behave badly?
3. What are some ways that parents can be punished for their children's behavior?

Unit 07 A Learning about the Topic

Should parents be punished when their children misbehave?

Read the passage and underline the main ideas. Track 19

One out of every three school children has been a victim of bullying. Schools typically respond to bullying by punishing the student responsible for it. Some schools, though, want to take a different approach. They suggest punishing misbehaving students along with their parents. Punishing parents for their children's bad behavior sounds like an effective solution in theory, but it could result in unforeseen drawbacks.

Even though it is true that parents bring their children into the world and are responsible for their upbringing, it is simply not possible for them to control their children's behavior at all times. Children are unique individuals. They have their own thoughts and **motivations**. If children choose to misbehave, it is not fair to punish parents for that. Likewise, children could misbehave for a variety of reasons. They may have physical or mental conditions such as attention-deficit disorder. Such conditions make it difficult for children to behave properly. They may still misbehave even if their parents are very caring and attentive. In any case, **implementing** a system of punishing parents would be a major challenge. It would require schools to work with law enforcement to create ways to punish parents. Such a system could meet a lot of **resistance** from parents, which could lead to lawsuits and other headaches for schools.

There are still many reasons to think punishing parents would be effective. Chiefly, it would force parents to be more responsible for their children. Because many parents these days work more and spend less time with their young ones, they may feel that their children's actions are not their fault. **Reprimanding** parents would correct this. Moreover, getting parents in trouble could be an opportunity to teach them how to be more effective parents. Part of the punishment could include having to take parenting classes on ways to encourage their children to be more attentive and respectful. From a legal standpoint, having parents receive **penalties** for the actions of their children should be straightforward. Parents are their children's legal guardians. This means that they can be held accountable for the behavior of their sons and daughters.

Vocabulary Check

Choose the correct word for each definition.

| motivation | implement | resistance | reprimand | penalty |

1. to criticize someone for his or her mistakes _____
2. to begin to use a plan _____
3. the act of giving someone a reason to do something _____
4. punishment for breaking a rule or law _____
5. refusal to accept something new _____

Comprehension Questions

Check the correct answer for each question.

1. What problems can children have because of attention-deficit disorder?
   - ☐ They may not listen to their parents when they get punished.
   - ☐ They may misbehave even though they have caring parents.

2. Why would it be difficult to create a system to punish parents?
   - ☐ Because schools would need to work with law enforcement
   - ☐ Because children can still choose to misbehave

3. How can parenting classes help improve student behavior?
   - ☐ Parents would learn ways to teach their children to pay attention and to be polite.
   - ☐ Parents would be reminded that they are responsible for their children's actions.

4. Why are parents legally responsible for their children?
   - ☐ Because their children live with them
   - ☐ Because they are their children's guardians

Questions for Debate

Think of and share ideas to explore the debatable issues in the article. Be sure to state your opinion clearly and to provide one supporting idea for each opinion.

1 Which types of punishments for students at your school do you think are the most effective?

It is my belief that _____

_____.

The reason I feel this way is _____

_____.

2 Is it reasonable to punish parents for their children's behavior? Explain.

My thinking is that _____

_____.

For instance, _____

_____.

3 Would it be better to punish parents every time their children break a rule or only when their children cause serious problems?

I believe that it would be better to _____

_____.

To be more specific, _____

_____.

4 Do you think most parents effectively discipline their children? Why or why not?

There is no doubt that _____

_____.

One example is _____

_____.

5 Instead of punishing parents, what can schools do to correct student misbehavior?

A better alternative might be _____

_____.

Allow me to explain further by mentioning that _____

_____.

Opinion Examples

Look at the opinion examples about the motion below and answer the questions.

Motion: It would be a mistake to punish parents for the actions of their children.

Opinion A Track 20

It is a ridiculous idea to get parents in trouble when their children misbehave at school. Certainly, parents play a major role in shaping their children's behavior, but they can't control them all of the time. Children are young and likely to act before thinking. You can't blame parents for that. Even enforcing parental punishments would be a major challenge. Schools alone could not do it. They would need the help of the police, courts, and attorneys. It would be a legal nightmare. Rather than punishing parents, schools should encourage them to become more involved in their children's education. At the same time, schools can teach students how to treat others and how to be well behaved.

Opinion B Track 21

Would you be surprised to learn that many of the worst-behaved students in my school are the ones with the worst parents? You shouldn't be. Much of children's misbehavior comes from poor parenting. Thus, the best solution is to punish parents. This would force parents to be more responsible for their children's actions. A lot of children behave badly because their parents are not involved in their lives. If parents could also be punished, you can be positive they would make sure their children behave well. Furthermore, parents are legally responsible for their children. If their children break the law, their parents can be punished. The same thing should happen when children break rules at school.

1 Underline the main idea of each opinion.

2 Which opinion is for the topic? Which one is against it?
- FOR: _____
- AGAINST: _____

3 What supporting ideas does each opinion give?
- Opinion A: _____
- Opinion B: _____

4 Create one more supporting idea for each argument.
- Opinion A: _____
- Opinion B: _____

Skills for Debate

Read and learn how to create effective rebuttals.

How Can You Create Effective Rebuttals?

A **rebuttal** is an argument that disproves an opponent's argument. In your debate, you give your rebuttal after the other team presents its argument. The first step to a good rebuttal is to point out a **flaw** in your opponent's argument. The most common flaws are **false statements, weak logic,** and **incorrect examples**. After mentioning the flaw in the other team's idea, you should **explain why** it is incorrect. Provide clear reasons to show why your rebuttal is more logical and correct. Some phrases to use in your rebuttal include "Your argument that… is wrong because" and "Our opponent's idea that… is incorrect due to the fact that…"

Practicing Debate Skills

Read each of the arguments below. Decide the flaw in each argument and write a rebuttal for it. Some words have been provided to help you.

1 Argument: Getting parents in trouble for their children's behavior is not legally possible.

Flaw: _____

Rebuttal: *Our opponent's argument that* _____
is flawed because _____

2 Argument: Punishing parents would force them to become better parents.

Flaw: _____

Rebuttal: *It is incorrect to assume that* _____
due to the fact that _____

3 Argument: Children with bad parents can never learn how to be good students.

Flaw: _____

Rebuttal: *The notion that* _____
does not make sense. The reason is _____

Unit 07 B Debating the Topic

Creating Your Debate

Motion: It would be a mistake to punish parents for the actions of their children.

What are your arguments? Get into two groups and plan for the debate. Decide whether your team is FOR (agree) or AGAINST (disagree) the motion. Then, create your ARE: Argument, Reason, and Example. Use the example arguments below and the research from your workbook to help create your arguments.

■ Example Arguments

FOR

Argument

Punishing parents would require extra resources that schools cannot afford.

Reason

Schools alone do not have the authority to punish parents. Doing so would require cooperation from law enforcement and courts. Unfortunately, many local governments already receive too little funding for schools. Trying to punish parents would be an expense they cannot afford.

Example

Many school districts are cutting back on teachers and buying fewer materials to save money. Trying to punish parents would present too many financial problems to try to do.

AGAINST

Argument

Punishments for parents would cause them to become more involved in their children's learning.

Reason

A large number of parents today feel that schools alone are responsible for teaching their children to behave well. The reality is that parents need to be involved in their children's education for it to be effective. A punishment system for parents can make this happen.

Example

A recent survey indicated that parents must cooperate with schools to make sure their children receive a proper social education.

Arguments FOR/AGAINST the Motion

ARGUMENT 1	ARGUMENT 2	ARGUMENT 3
Argument	**Argument**	**Argument**
Reason	**Reason**	**Reason**
Example	**Example**	**Example**

Actual Debate

Now, it's time to debate. Use the flow chart below to help you organize the debate.
The introductory expressions have been provided to help you. Put your arguments in logical order and make clear rebuttals to the opposing team's arguments.

Agree Opening Statement
It is our central belief that _____.

Agree Argument 1
We would like to begin by pointing out that _____.

Rebuttal 1
To refute your argument, we will mention that _____.

Agree Argument 2
The next point we would like to bring up is _____.

Rebuttal 2
Once again, we have to disagree. We think that _____.

Agree Argument 3
Our third argument is _____.

Agree Closing Statement
Despite our opponent's arguments, we still believe that _____.

Disagree Opening Statement
As for our team, we are positive that _____.

Rebuttal 1
Your contention that _____ is flawed because _____.

Disagree Argument 1
Our starting argument is _____.

Rebuttal 2
We disagree once again. The fact is _____.

Disagree Argument 2
Our second supporting idea is _____.

Rebuttal 3
To us, it seems that _____ is not the case since _____.

Disagree Argument 3
To give our final point, consider that _____.

Disagree Closing Statement
To summarize, we hold that _____.

Sum Up the Debate

Finish the debate summary.

AGREEING SIDE'S ARGUMENT

Today's debate motion was _____.

The primary argument of the first team was _____.

First of all, _____.

More specifically, _____
_____.

Next, they explained _____.

To share their supporting arguments, _____
_____.

Their last point was _____.

The idea that _____
_____ illustrated their claim.

DISAGREEING SIDE'S ARGUMENT

The second team felt the opposite. Their main idea was _____
_____.

The first reason they mentioned was _____.

This was supported by _____
_____.

Second, they contented _____.

To share their evidence, they said _____
_____.

They wrapped up by arguing that _____.

For example, _____
_____.

87

Unit 08 Studying Abroad

A. Discuss the following questions as a class.
1. What do you see in the picture above?
2. What do you notice about the children in this picture?
3. How can studying abroad be different from studying in one's home country?

B. Answer the following questions with a partner.
1. What are some reasons that parents send their children abroad to study?
2. Have you studied abroad? If so, how was your experience? If not, would you like to?
3. What problems can occur if children study abroad without their parents?

Unit 08 A Learning about the Topic

Should children study abroad away from their families?

Read the passage and underline the main ideas. Track 22

Millions of students from countries all over the world attend college abroad. In many countries, getting a degree from a foreign university is considered essential for success. As the world is becoming more competitive, some parents are now sending their children to other countries to study during middle school, elementary school, and even kindergarten. For these parents, the benefits of studying abroad are **considerable**.

The main purpose of parents sending their children abroad to study is to help them learn English and other languages. Many nations place great **emphasis** on foreign language skills. Sending children abroad when they are young will ensure that they learn another language fluently. Research shows that children learn foreign languages best between the ages of 8 and 12. Students can also be exposed to different learning methods by studying abroad. For instance, American schools often place great emphasis on creative thinking and activities. This can help students develop their critical-thinking skills better than they could by studying in their home countries. Living abroad also helps children become more **resourceful** and independent. They have to adjust to an environment that is very different from the one in their home country.

These advantages can also present major challenges for children studying abroad. Students will be studying in classes conducted in a foreign language. Because of this, they can quickly fall behind academically. Differences in teaching methods can present similar problems for students. The material students study in a foreign country may be more difficult than that curriculum from their home country. These students may **struggle** to keep up. The opposite case is also problematic. When students return to their home countries, they may have fallen behind their classmates. Most pressingly, students studying abroad are forced to be away from their family and native culture. They can suffer from **anxiety** and loneliness. Even children who go abroad with their mothers and siblings can suffer an emotional toll.

Vocabulary Check

Choose the correct word for each definition.

| considerable | emphasis | resourceful | struggle | anxiety |

1 to try very hard to do something difficult   _____
2 special attention given to something   _____
3 fear or nervousness about something that might happen _____
4 able to deal with difficult situations and to find solutions _____
5 large in size, amount, or quantity   _____

Comprehension Questions

Check the correct answer for each question.

1 Why are parents sending their young children abroad to study?
   ☐ Because studying abroad is considered necessary for success
   ☐ Because the world is becoming a more competitive place

2 What is true about learning foreign languages?
   ☐ It is necessary in order to find a job as an adult.
   ☐ It is better to learn them between the ages of 8 and 12.

3 How can children develop greater critical-thinking skills by studying abroad?
   ☐ They would be educated through various learning methods.
   ☐ They would be required to do creative activities in school.

4 What problems could children face by studying in other countries? Choose TWO correct answers.
   ☐ Being treated differently than other children
   ☐ Studying a more difficult curriculum
   ☐ Learning a new foreign language
   ☐ Being away from their family and culture

Questions for Debate

Think of and share ideas to explore the debatable issues in the article. Be sure to state your opinion clearly and to provide one supporting idea for each opinion.

1 What important skills can children learn by studying in another country?

Some of the important skills children learn are _____
_____.

These are important because _____
_____.

2 Is it true that children become more independent by studying abroad?

My feeling about this matter is _____
_____.

To share an example, _____
_____.

3 Do you think parents should send their children to live abroad alone, or should they have to go with their children?

I think parents should _____
_____.

I feel this way since _____
_____.

4 What academic problems can occur due to differences in what children study in school?

These problems can include _____
_____.

These matter because _____
_____.

5 What alternatives do parents have other than sending their children abroad to study?

One option is _____
_____.

The reason this is better is _____
_____.

Opinion Examples

Look at the opinion examples about the motion below and answer the questions.

Motion: Studying abroad provides many important benefits for children.

Opinion A Track 23

When I was 9 years old, I studied in Canada for a year, and I'm glad I did. Studying abroad has given me a lot of benefits. The most obvious benefit is that I was able to learn English fluently. Now I can speak English just like a native speaker. If I had never studied abroad, I would never be this good at English. Another important benefit of studying in Canada is that I experienced a very different learning environment. Schools in my home country make students memorize a lot of facts. In Canada, we did a lot more projects and had to use more creative thinking. This helped me build my critical-thinking skills.

Opinion B Track 24

There are some advantages of studying abroad, but I still think young students should stay in their home countries to study. For one, there is serious culture shock. Every country has its own unique culture. This includes everything from the type of houses people live in to what information children study in school. Young children have a very hard time dealing with such a huge change to their environment. At the same time, studying abroad often means being away from family. When we are young, we need the love and support of our family. But when students are thousands of kilometers from home, this isn't possible.

1 Underline the main idea of each opinion.

2 Which opinion is for the topic? Which one is against it?

- FOR: _____
- AGAINST: _____

3 What supporting ideas does each opinion give?

- Opinion A: _____
- Opinion B: _____

4 Create one more supporting idea for each argument.

- Opinion A: _____
- Opinion B: _____

Skills for Debate

Read and learn how to create effective rebuttals.

How Can You Create Effective Rebuttals?

In addition to pointing out flaws in the other team's arguments, **rebuttals** give you the chance to **highlight the advantages of your arguments**. One strategy is to explain how the **flaws in your opponent's arguments are benefits for your argument**. This is easiest if your arguments directly contradict one another. Alternatively, you could mention how your argument is **more likely to be correct**. Compare how likely your argument is to be true compared to your opponent's idea. In both cases, you should introduce your ideas with phrases such as, "The weaknesses of their argument become more apparent when you consider that…" and "Our opponent's argument that… actually strengthens our point because…"

Practicing Debate Skills

Read the arguments below. The first argument is for your side, and the second argument is your opponent's statement. Use them to create rebuttals and to give advantages for your arguments.

1 **Your Argument:** Children can become fluent in another language by studying abroad.

   Opponent's Argument: It is possible for children to learn foreign languages in their home country.

   Rebuttal: *The other team contends that* _____.

   The problem with this way of thinking is that _____.

   Advantages of Your Argument: *Our argument is actually superior because* _____.

2 **Your Argument:** There are many emotional problems that can happen when children study abroad away from their family.

   Opponent's Argument: It is possible for families to live abroad together.

   Rebuttal: *Your notion that* _____

   does not make sense because _____.

   Advantages of Your Argument: *As we see it, it would be better to* _____.

Unit 08 B Debating the Topic

Creating Your Debate

Motion: Studying abroad provides many important benefits for children.

What are your arguments? Get into two groups and plan for the debate. Decide whether your team is FOR (agree) or AGAINST (disagree) the motion. Then, create your ARE: Argument, Reason, and Example. Use the example arguments below and the research from your workbook to help create your arguments.

■ Example Arguments

FOR

Argument

Going to school in another country broadens students' views of the world.

Reason

The world today is a globalized place, and it is important to understand other cultures and perspectives. Studying abroad at a young age gives children special insights into how people in other places live and think.

Example

Children who have studied abroad are more likely to try new activities and less likely to have a negative view of foreigners.

AGAINST

Argument

Students can have a hard time adapting to school systems in other countries.

Reason

Each nation has its own educational system. Sometimes there is a great difference between the way students are taught, how much they have to study, etc. This can make it hard for students to do well in school when they are trying to integrate into a new culture.

Example

My friend Alex is usually a great student. But when he went to school in England, his grades fell because he was not used to writing essays and doing group activities.

■ Arguments FOR/AGAINST the Motion

ARGUMENT 1

Argument

Reason

Example

ARGUMENT 2

Argument

Reason

Example

ARGUMENT 3

Argument

Reason

Example

Actual Debate

Now, it's time to debate. Use the flow chart below to help you organize the debate.
The introductory expressions have been provided to help you. Put your arguments in logical order and make clear rebuttals to the opposing team's arguments.

Agree Opening Statement
We, the members of the pro team, believe that _____.

Disagree Opening Statement
From our perspective, the drawbacks of ____ _____ outweigh the benefits.

Agree Argument 1
To begin with, _____
_____
_____
_____
_____.

Rebuttal 1
It is incorrect for you to claim that _____
_____ since _____
_____.

Disagree Argument 1
One problem with _____ is
_____.

Rebuttal 1
You claim that _____
_____, yet we feel that _____
_____.

Rebuttal 2
You argument that _____
_____ is wrong since
_____.

Agree Argument 2
We also support this motion because ____
_____.

Disagree Argument 2
Next, let us mention that _____
_____.

Rebuttal 2
You said that _____
_____.
However, we believe that _____
_____.

Rebuttal 3
The other team is mistaken again. The fact is
_____,
_____
_____.

Agree Argument 3
Our last point is _____
_____.

Disagree Argument 3
Last, but not least, _____
_____.

Agree Closing Statement
In the end, we contend that _____
_____.

Disagree Closing Statement
To sum up, _____
_____.

Sum Up the Debate

Finish the debate summary.

AGREEING SIDE'S ARGUMENT

The topic of this debate was _____.

The pro team supported the notion that _____.

First of all, they believed that _____.

Their supporting evidence was _____
_____.

Next, they posited that _____.

For instance, _____
_____.

Their third point was _____.

The example they mentioned was _____
_____.

DISAGREEING SIDE'S ARGUMENT

In contrast, the con team argued that _____
_____.

They started off by saying that _____.

Their example was _____
_____.

The second point they made was _____.

For instance, _____
_____.

The final reason they mentioned was _____.

_____ was given to prove this point.

97

Chapter 5

Creating Closing Speeches

Unit 09 Universal Healthcare

Unit 10 Nuclear Weapons

Unit 09: Universal Healthcare

WARM-UP

A. Discuss the following questions as a class.

1. What do you see in the picture above?
2. Why do you think money is included in the picture?
3. What are some reasons that healthcare costs a lot of money?

B. Answer the following questions with a partner.

1. Do people in your family usually go to the doctor when they are sick? Why or why not?
2. How much do you think one visit to the doctor's should cost?
3. What are some reasons that governments should offer healthcare to their citizens?

Unit 09 A Learning about the Topic

Should governments provide healthcare to all their citizens?

Read the passage and underline the main ideas.   Track 25

The first modern universal healthcare system was introduced by the Soviet Union in 1937. The country provided its citizens with medical and dental care along with medical supplies at no cost. Today, nearly 60 countries, including Denmark, Japan, and Germany, provide universal healthcare to their citizens. Most people agree that individuals should have greater access to healthcare. Still, universal healthcare remains a hotly contended issue.

A common fear is that universal healthcare will decrease the quality of medical services. Since many people will want to get medical treatment, doctors will spend less time **diagnosing** each patient. This will lead to long wait times and potential misdiagnoses. We can already see this in the United Kingdom and Canada. Furthermore, some medical procedures could become more expensive. In most nations, universal healthcare covers **routine** medical checkups and dental work. However, major surgeries are not covered. For people who need these major surgeries, having private medical insurance can actually be cheaper. Lastly, the money spent on young healthy people in universal healthcare systems is wasted. A number of countries fund their universal healthcare for all citizens. For young people, though, the money is not needed because they are usually healthier and rarely need to visit the doctor.

It is important to keep in mind that access to healthcare is a **fundamental** human right. This is explained in Article 25 of the Universal Declaration of Human Rights. Having free healthcare affords citizens a better quality of life. They can work more and earn more money since they suffer fewer health problems. They also live longer. Additionally, a lot of evidence **indicates** that universal healthcare actually makes costs go down. The United States is the only developed country that does not provide universal healthcare. Over 53 percent of the population pays their own health insurance costs. Nonetheless, the country spends far more on healthcare than any other nation. The lack of free public health care means higher prices for **patients** and makes proper health care too expensive for many to afford.

Vocabulary Check

Choose the correct word for each definition.

| diagnose | routine | fundamental | indicate | patient |

1 to recognize a disease by examining someone _____
2 to show something _____
3 a person who receives medical care from a doctor _____
4 done normally as part of a process _____
5 relating to the basic part of something _____

Comprehension Questions

Check the correct answer for each question.

1 What is the definition of universal healthcare?
 □ Providing medical and dental care at no cost for all citizens
 □ Providing low-cost medical care for sick people

2 How can free medical care lead to lower quality service?
 □ Because major surgeries will not be paid for by the government
 □ Because doctors will spend less time diagnosing each patient

3 What is the problem of providing free healthcare to young people?
 □ They are generally healthy and do not need to visit the doctor.
 □ They do not have enough money to pay their own insurance costs.

4 What is the healthcare situation in the United States?
 □ The lack of free healthcare forces healthcare providers to lower their prices.
 □ People need health insurance because there is no universal healthcare.

Questions for Debate

Think of and share ideas to explore the debatable issues in the article. Be sure to state your opinion clearly and to provide one supporting idea for each opinion.

1 How can individuals benefit from free universal healthcare?

I believe that _____

_____.

This is due to the fact that _____

_____.

2 How can nations benefit when they offer free universal healthcare?

They can primarily benefit from _____

_____.

For example, _____

_____.

3 Is it better to require citizens to participate in universal healthcare, or should they have the option not to participate?

My feeling about the matter is _____

_____.

To go into more detail, _____

_____.

4 Do you believe that access to healthcare is a fundamental human right? Why or why not?

From my point of view, it seems that _____

_____.

More specifically, _____

_____.

5 Aside from free universal healthcare, what are some other ways governments can make healthcare more accessible for citizens?

A better alternative might be _____

_____.

For instance, _____

_____.

Opinion Examples

Look at the opinion examples about the motion below and answer the questions.

Motion: Providing free national healthcare would be a mistake.

Opinion A Track 26

We need free universal healthcare now. Being able to get medical treatment has a major impact on people's quality of life. If we can't go to the doctor when we are sick, we can develop serious illnesses and even die early. This is one reason universal healthcare is needed. Another reason is that it is the government's job to care for its people. The government already provides many other services for education, transportation, water, and more. Healthcare is arguably more important than any of these. It is just irresponsible for people who can't afford to go to the doctor to have to stay sick. The government has to step up and make sure all citizens have healthy, happy lives.

Opinion B Track 27

At some point in our lives, healthcare becomes hugely important. However, not everybody needs or wants national healthcare. That's why I think universal healthcare is unnecessary. First of all, it would be a waste of money. The government would have to spend billions of dollars each year on a service that not all citizens would use. It would be better to use the money to provide benefits everybody needs, such as housing and job training. Even if cost is not a problem, the quality of the healthcare would be. Free healthcare would mean that more people would take trips to the doctor. This would lead to longer waiting times and lower quality service.

1 Underline the main idea of each opinion.

2 Which opinion is for the topic? Which one is against it?
- FOR: _____
- AGAINST: _____

3 What supporting ideas does each opinion give?
- Opinion A: _____
- Opinion B: _____

4 Create one more supporting idea for each argument.
- Opinion A: _____
- Opinion B: _____

Skills for Debate

Read and learn how to create closing speeches.

How Can You Create Closing Speeches?

The **closing speech** is the final part of your debate. It is your last chance to make an impression on the judges and the other team. Closing speeches generally have two parts. The first part is the **summary**. This is where you give an **overview** of your team's **central argument** and **supporting ideas**. You should **paraphrase** your team's arguments. It is also a good idea to provide an additional **example** for your team's point of view. This will help the judges understand your arguments better.

Practicing Debate Skills

Use the following debate motion and arguments to create a closing speech summary. Paraphrase the ideas and add one extra piece of evidence. Some words have been provided to help you.

Motion: Governments should be responsible for providing healthcare to their citizens.

FOR Arguments:
- Governments must offer necessary services for citizens.
- Offering free healthcare would help people live better lives.
- Workers could have greater productivity with free healthcare.

Closing Summary: Our central opinion about this topic remains _____.

For our initial argument, we stated that _____.

We went on to explain that _____.

The final argument we gave was _____.

AGAINST Arguments:
- Providing healthcare at no cost would be too expensive.
- The quality of service would decrease greatly with free healthcare.
- Not all people need healthcare anyway.

Closing Summary: To restate our point of view, _____.

The first argument we shared was _____.

For our next point, we said that _____.

Finally, we contended that _____.

Unit 09 B Debating the Topic

Creating Your Debate

Motion: Providing free national healthcare would be a mistake.

What are your arguments? Get into two groups and plan for the debate. Decide whether your team is FOR (agree) or AGAINST (disagree) the motion. Then, create your ARE: Argument, Reason, and Example. Use the example arguments below and the research from your workbook to help create your arguments.

■ Example Arguments

FOR

Argument

Free healthcare would be wasted on millions of people.

Reason

Elderly and low-income people need free government healthcare because they cannot otherwise afford treatment. However, younger people do not need it because they are rarely sick. In addition, people with higher incomes often prefer to pay for their own healthcare to get better service.

Example

A recent survey of people in their 20s found that less than a third of them reported going to the doctor more than two times a year. The reasons are that they are young and generally healthy.

AGAINST

Argument

Access to healthcare is a fundamental human right.

Reason

It is generally believed that all people have the right to be healthy. Governments must be willing and able to ensure the health of their citizens by providing healthcare services where they are needed.

Example

Article 25 of the Universal Declaration of Human Rights clearly states that all people should be allowed to receive medical treatment when they need to do so.

■ Arguments FOR/AGAINST the Motion

ARGUMENT 1	ARGUMENT 2	ARGUMENT 3
Argument	**Argument**	**Argument**
Reason	**Reason**	**Reason**
Example	**Example**	**Example**

Actual Debate

Now, it's time to debate. Use the flow chart below to help you organize the debate.
The introductory expressions have been provided to help you. Put your arguments in logical order and make clear rebuttals to the opposing team's arguments.

Agree Opening Statement
Our opinion about this motion is _____.

Agree Argument 1
First of all, _____
_____
_____
_____.

Rebuttal 1
Despite your argument that _____
_____, we contend that _____
_____.

Agree Argument 2
The point we want to make is _____
_____.

Rebuttal 2
Unfortunately, we must disagree. In reality, _____
_____
_____.

Agree Argument 3
Our third and final argument is _____
_____.

Agree Closing Statement
To sum up, we believe that _____
_____.

Disagree Opening Statement
In contrast, we believe that _____
_____.

Rebuttal 1
Our opponents believe that _____
_____.

This is false because _____
_____.

Disagree Argument 1
As for our first argument, we feel that _____
_____.

Rebuttal 2
You wrongly assert that _____
_____.

Disagree Argument 2
We would also like you to think about how _____
_____
_____.

Rebuttal 3
Despite your opinion that _____
_____, we contend that _____
_____.

Disagree Argument 3
As for our last argument, _____
_____.

Disagree Closing Statement
It is our overall opinion that _____
_____.

Sum Up the Debate

Finish the debate summary.

AGREEING SIDE'S ARGUMENT

The motion for today's debate was _____.

The first team argued that _____.

To begin with, they claimed that _____.

More specifically, they stated that _____
_____.

Next, they posited that _____.

Their support was _____
_____.

Their third reason was _____.

For instance, _____
_____.

DISAGREEING SIDE'S ARGUMENT

In contrast, the other team believed that _____
_____.

The first argument they mentioned was _____.

To justify this, they explained that _____
_____.

Their second point was _____.

The example they gave was _____
_____.

Lastly, they posited that _____.

In detail, they went over _____
_____.

Unit 10 Nuclear Weapons

WARM-UP

A. Discuss the following questions as a class.

1. What do you see in the picture above?
2. Why do you think the man is wearing a mask?
3. What are the main dangers of using nuclear weapons in a war?

B. Answer the following questions with a partner.

1. Which countries do you know that have nuclear weapons? List all of them.
2. Do you believe that having nuclear weapons makes the world safer? Explain.
3. How can nuclear weapons help end wars more quickly?

Unit 10 A Learning about the Topic

Should nations be allowed to keep nuclear weapons?

Read the passage and underline the main ideas. Track 28

Fat Man and Little Boy were the only two nuclear weapons ever used during a time of war. They annihilated the cities of Nagasaki and Hiroshima. Tens of thousands of people died. The devastating power of nuclear weapons can cause tremendous amounts of death and **destruction** and can seriously damage the environment. Simultaneously, nuclear weapons are a highly effective way to prevent wars and save millions of lives.

By having nuclear weapons, governments can maintain their national freedom. A country that has nuclear weapons is feared and respected by other nations of the world. They know that invading a country with nukes could lead to serious consequences. It is in this regard that atomic weapons allow nations to maintain their **sovereignty**. For a similar reason, nuclear bombs can promote world peace. The weapons deter nations from fighting with each other. This is what happened during the Cold War. The United States and Soviet Union were enemies, but they never fought any battles. This was due to the fact that each country knew the other side had nuclear weapons. If a war were to **break out**, it would end quickly. A nation would only have to drop one or two atomic bombs to end the fighting.

Nevertheless, the drawbacks of nuclear weapons cannot be **ignored**. The nuclear weapons of today are thousands of times more powerful than Fat Man and Llittle Boy were. A single bomb could destroy even the world's largest cities and kill millions of people. The high levels of nuclear radiation released by the bombs would make the explosion sites unlivable for decades. These dramatic, long-lasting effects are not worth ending a war in an instant. One must also consider that effect that weapons of mass destruction can have on national leaders. Such weapons can lead them to do dangerous actions that harm their own people and possibly the entire world. North Korea is a prime example of this. Their leaders continue to **defy** the nations of the world on issues such as human rights because they claim to have nuclear bombs.

Vocabulary Check

Choose the correct word for each definition.

| destruction | sovereignty | break out | ignore | defy |

1 to do nothing in response to someone or something _____
2 to refuse to obey _____
3 to begin happening suddenly _____
4 damaging something completely so it no longer exists _____
5 unlimited power over a country _____

Comprehension Questions

Check the correct answer for each question.

1 What is true about nations that have nuclear weapons?
- ☐ Other nations fear and respect them more.
- ☐ They are more likely to attack other nations.

2 Why did the United States and the Soviet Union not fight during the Cold War?
- ☐ Because they wanted to promote world peace
- ☐ Because they knew both of them had nuclear weapons

3 What are the long-term effects of nuclear weapons?
- ☐ They can destroy the world's largest cities and kill millions.
- ☐ The nuclear radiation makes areas unlivable for decades.

4 How can having nuclear weapons affect national leaders?
- ☐ It can cause them to do actions that are dangerous and destructive.
- ☐ It leads them to defy the other nations of the world on important issues.

Questions for Debate

Think of and share ideas to explore the debatable issues in the article. Be sure to state your opinion clearly and to provide one supporting idea for each opinion.

1 Do you think your country should have nuclear weapons? Why or why not?

It is my opinion that _____
_____.

I feel this way because _____
_____.

2 Why do you think only two nuclear bombs have ever been used during wartime? Explain.

I believe that _____
_____.

To go into more detail, _____
_____.

3 How can dropping atomic bombs help end wars more quickly?

From my point of view, it seems that _____
_____.

For instance, _____
_____.

4 Do you think it will be possible for all the nations in the world to get rid of their nuclear weapons? Why or why not?

My feeling is that _____
_____.

One example is _____
_____.

5 How else can nations solve their problems without using atomic weapons to fight wars?

A better solution could be _____
_____.

I believe this would be better since _____
_____.

Opinion Examples

Look at the opinion examples about the motion below and answer the questions.

Motion: Nuclear weapons help make the world a safer place.

Opinion A Track 29

Nuclear weapons are an incredible technology, one that should have not been developed. To ensure world safety, the governments of the world need to get rid of their nuclear weapons as soon as possible. For one, the destructive power of nuclear weapons is too great. Each atomic bomb dropped on Japan killed tens of thousands of people. Today's nuclear weapons are so powerful that millions of people could die. Why would any country need such destructive power? More worrying is that terrorists or dictators could get nuclear weapons. With these weapons of mass destruction, terrorist groups could hold world governments hostage unless their demands are met.

Opinion B Track 30

Nuclear weapons are extremely destructive. This is exactly why they should be used to keep world peace. People fear the power of nuclear weapons. National leaders know that starting a war with countries that have atomic weapons could cause serious destruction. For this reason, nuclear weapons actually decrease the chances of war from occurring. Even if war does break out, nuclear weapons can help end the fighting quickly. Look at what happened in World War II. The Japanese government refused to surrender until the U.S. military dropped two atomic bombs on the country. Yes, lots of people died, but it was better than having the war continue for many years.

1. Underline the main idea of each opinion.

2. Which opinion is for the topic? Which one is against it?
   - FOR: _____
   - AGAINST: _____

3. What supporting ideas does each opinion give?
   - Opinion A: _____
   - Opinion B: _____

4. Create one more supporting idea for each argument.
   - Opinion A: _____
   - Opinion B: _____

Skills for Debate

Read and learn how to create closing speeches.

How Can You Create Closing Speeches?

The last part of a closing speech is called the **final shot**. In your final shot, you should make an **emotional statement**. Talk directly to the listeners by using the word "you" in your speech. The final shot should **attack the other team's central argument** or **explain why people must follow your argument**. Some good phrases to use include "I hope that you now realize how absurd (*the other team's argument*) really is" along with "You must remember that (*your team's argument*) is the best course of action."

Practicing Debate Skills

Read the following arguments. Create final shot speeches for each idea. First, restate your argument, and then make an emotional statement. Use the words in the idea boxes to help you.

Argument: Nuclear weapons should be banned because they are far too destructive.

Idea Box

future of the world depends on banning nuclear weapons / nuclear weapons are simply too powerful to allow / allowing atomic weapons could lead to the end of the human race

Final Shot: *It is our hope that you know realize why* _____

because _____

_____ *Thank you.*

Argument: Nuclear weapons are necessary to prevent greater death and destruction.

Idea Box

the only good war is one that never happens / causing a few thousand deaths is better than causing several million / nuclear weapons are the only way to stop evil in our world

Final Shot: *I am sure you know understand that* _____

The fact remains that _____

_____ *Thank you.*

Unit 10 B Debating the Topic

Creating Your Debate

Motion: Nuclear weapons help make the world a safer place.

What are your arguments? Get into two groups and plan for the debate. Decide whether your team is FOR (agree) or AGAINST (disagree) the motion. Then, create your ARE: Argument, Reason, and Example. Use the example arguments below and the research from your workbook to help create your arguments.

- **Example Arguments**

FOR

Argument

Nuclear weapons can prevent large wars from occurring.

Reason

National leaders realize the incredible power of nuclear weapons. They would not risk starting a war with a country that has nuclear weapons. The leaders know that doing so could lead to the end of their government, and even the whole world.

Example

The Cold War between the United States and the Soviet Union never led to large-scale fighting because each country knew the other side had atomic weapons.

AGAINST

Argument

Nations can solve their problems with discussion, not the nuclear destruction.

Reason

We live in a world of globalization. This means that all the nations of the world rely on one another for trade, education, and more. In our world, war is no longer needed. Global leaders can discuss their problems in diplomatic ways.

Example

The number of trade agreements between nations is at an all time high. This shows how much the world's nations rely on each other today. Problems should be solved by talking, not war.

- **Arguments FOR/AGAINST the Motion**

ARGUMENT 1	ARGUMENT 2	ARGUMENT 3
Argument	**Argument**	**Argument**
Reason	**Reason**	**Reason**
Example	**Example**	**Example**

Actual Debate

Now, it's time to debate. Use the flow chart below to help you organize the debate.
The introductory expressions have been provided to help you. Put your arguments in logical order and make clear rebuttals to the opposing team's arguments.

Agree Opening Statement
Our stance on the issue of _____
is that _____
_____.

Agree Argument 1
The first point we will make is _____
_____
_____
_____
_____.

Rebuttal 1
It is wrong to assume that _____
since _____.

Agree Argument 2
Second, we feel that _____
_____
_____.

Rebuttal 2
The idea that _____
_____
is wrong because _____
_____.

Agree Argument 3
The final argument we have is _____
_____
_____.

Agree Closing Statement
Our overall opinion remains that _____
_____.

Disagree Opening Statement
Unlike our opponents, it is clear to us that _____
_____
_____.

Rebuttal 1
Your statement that _____
_____ is flawed because
_____.

Disagree Argument 1
Our first argument is _____
_____.

Rebuttal 2
You argue that _____
_____,
yet _____.

Disagree Argument 2
The next reason we oppose this topic is _____
_____.

Rebuttal 3
We disagree that _____
_____ and feel that _____
_____.

Disagree Argument 3
Last, it is our conviction that _____
_____.

Disagree Closing Statement
In conclusion, it is clear that _____
_____.

Sum Up the Debate

Finish the debate summary.

AGREEING SIDE'S ARGUMENT

Our debate today dealt with _____.

The first team supported the topic and stated that _____.

First of all, they claimed that _____.

Their example was _____
_____.

Next, they mentioned that _____.

To go into more detail, _____
_____.

The closing argument they gave was _____.

Specifically, _____
_____.

DISAGREEING SIDE'S ARGUMENT

To oppose the motion, the other team stated that _____
_____.

The first reason they opposed the motion was _____.

To elaborate, they stated that _____
_____.

Second, they posited that _____.

Their evidence was _____
_____.

As for their third argument, it was _____.

For instance, _____
_____.

Instilling Knowledge and Skills
for Thoughtful Debate

DEBATE Pro

Book 4

Jonathan S. McClelland

Workbook

DEBATE Pro
Book 4

Workbook

Contents

How to Use This Book _4

- **Unit 01** Outlawing Violent Sports _6
- **Unit 02** Part-Time Jobs for Teenagers _10
- **Unit 03** Teaching Practical Subjects _14
- **Unit 04** Child Curfews _18
- **Unit 05** Internet Censorship _22
- **Unit 06** Free Public Transportation _26
- **Unit 07** Punishing Parents _30
- **Unit 08** Studying Abroad _34
- **Unit 09** Universal Healthcare _38
- **Unit 10** Nuclear Weapons _42

How to Use This Book

Overview

The workbook is intended to supplement the main book both during class and for homework. It provides space for students to take notes during class and to do additional research outside of class.

Introduction for each section

Organizing Ideas

This part requires students to analyze the reading passage from the main book and write down each of the arguments and examples for and against the topic.

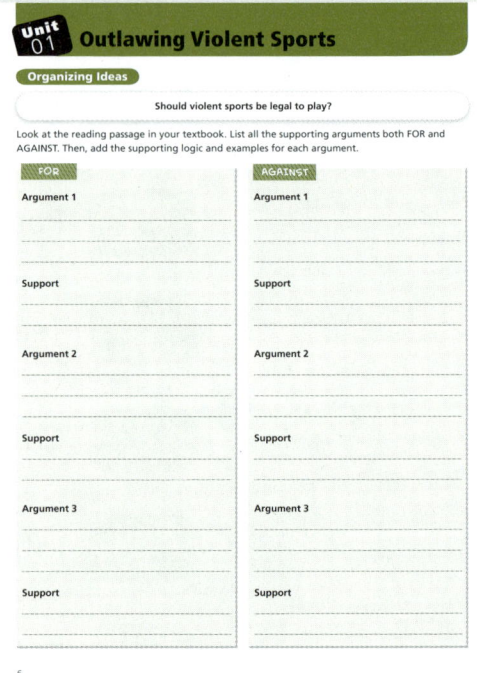

Making Supporting Examples

This section helps students develop their skills in making examples. In each book, five types of examples are explained: statistics, expert opinions, facts, academic studies, and personal opinions.

Additional Research

This section provides students with additional information about the topic based on the type of example explained in the previous section. The information is followed by four brief comprehension questions. Sample phrases are provided to help students create their answers.

Your Research

In this section, students are asked to do additional research outside of class. They are encouraged to find information from magazines, newspapers, or academic websites and to write or tape the material in the space provided. Based on the information they find, students are asked to create four additional examples which they can use during their debate.

Debate Note-Taking

This section provides space which students can use to take notes during the debate.

Peer Evaluation

This part requires students to evaluate their peers' debate performance. Eight criteria are provided along with a ten-point scale for each criterion with a total maximum score of eighty points for each student.

Unit 01 Outlawing Violent Sports

Organizing Ideas

Should violent sports be legal to play?

Look at the reading passage in your textbook. List all the supporting arguments both FOR and AGAINST. Then, add the supporting logic and examples for each argument.

FOR	AGAINST
Argument 1	**Argument 1**
Support	**Support**
Argument 2	**Argument 2**
Support	**Support**
Argument 3	**Argument 3**
Support	**Support**

Making Supporting Examples: Expert Opinions

Expert opinions are usually the ideas and opinions of experts in any given field. Experts are typically people such as professors, doctors, and business managers. Most experts base their opinions on their years of experience doing research and working in their fields. Below are some expert opinions related to the topic of violent sports.

Additional Research

Before starting your argument, let's do some extra research on the topic. Read the expert opinions about violent sports.

Dr. Joseph Stein, Medical Doctor

As a sports medicine doctor, I always recommend that my patients get physical exercise. Some of the best sports are swimming, jogging, and tennis. There are, however, some physical activities I would never recommend. Violent sports, also known as contact sports, such as football, boxing, and wrestling cause most of the sports injuries I deal with. Yes, there are safety regulations to keep players safe, but this does not mean there will never be any accidents. Torn muscles and broken bones are serious enough, but violent sports can even lead to concussions, which can cause permanent injuries. If you want to exercise, do not play contact sports. Your body will thank you.

Phil Madden, Football Coach

In all my years of coaching, I have never had a player be seriously injured on the field. Sure, players get cuts and bruises, but those heal quickly. The worst injuries have been broken bones, but even in these cases, the players were able to be back playing in almost no time. The fact is that even violent sports like football are safer than the critics argue. We take every possible safety precaution to reduce the chance of injury. Our players wear strong helmets and thick body padding. The chance of suffering a serious injury while playing football is very low while the chance of becoming physically fit is very high.

Work with a partner and answer the following questions. Phrases have been provided to help you.

1 What sports does Dr. Stein recommend that patients play to stay healthy?

→ *He recommends that patients* _____.

2 How does the doctor feel about the safety regulations in violent sports?

→ *He feels that* _____.

3 What is the most serious injury players on Coach Madden's team have experienced?

→ *The most serious injury has been* _____.

4 What is the coach's overall opinion of football?

→ *His overall opinion is* _____.

Your Research

Find an article about outlawing violent sports from a magazine, newspaper, or academic website. Paste or tape the article in your workbook in the space below.

Paste or Tape Your Research Article Here

Read your article and write four specific examples or pieces of evidence you can use for your debate. Try to include different types of examples, including opinion polls, statistics, academic studies, and general facts.

- _____
- _____
- _____
- _____

Debate Note-Taking

Use this page to take notes about the opposing team's arguments during the debate.

Note-Taking

Peer Evaluation

Read the assessment criteria and objectively evaluate your peers on a scale from 1 to 10.

CRITERIA	Name				
Understands the subject well	/10	/10	/10	/10	/10
Supports opinion with clear logic and examples	/10	/10	/10	/10	/10
Introduces opinions with appropriate connectors (In my view, I agree, For example, etc.)	/10	/10	/10	/10	/10
Uses a variety of vocabulary and expressions	/10	/10	/10	/10	/10
Accurately uses a variety of grammatical structures	/10	/10	/10	/10	/10
Does not monopolize the conversation and lets other people express themselves	/10	/10	/10	/10	/10
Listens attentively and respects other people's opinions	/10	/10	/10	/10	/10
Is able to accept criticism without becoming upset	/10	/10	/10	/10	/10
TOTAL SCORE	/80	/80	/80	/80	/80

Unit 02 Part-Time Jobs for Teenagers

Organizing Ideas

Should teenagers be allowed to work at part-time jobs?

Look at the reading passage in your textbook. List all the supporting arguments both FOR and AGAINST. Then, add the supporting logic and examples for each argument.

FOR	AGAINST
Argument 1	**Argument 1**
_____	_____
_____	_____
_____	_____
Support	**Support**
_____	_____
_____	_____
_____	_____
Argument 2	**Argument 2**
_____	_____
_____	_____
_____	_____
Support	**Support**
_____	_____
_____	_____
_____	_____
Argument 3	**Argument 3**
_____	_____
_____	_____
_____	_____
Support	**Support**
_____	_____
_____	_____
_____	_____

Making Supporting Examples: Statistics

Statistics are facts based on numbers. They are usually created by governments, universities, news organizations, and companies. Statistics often show the number of people, companies, and nations that agree with a certain opinion or policy. To show these numbers, statistics can include percentages, populations, and points. Below are some statistics related to the topic of part-time jobs for teenagers.

Additional Research

Before starting your argument, let's do some extra research on the topic. Read the statistics about part-time jobs for teenagers.

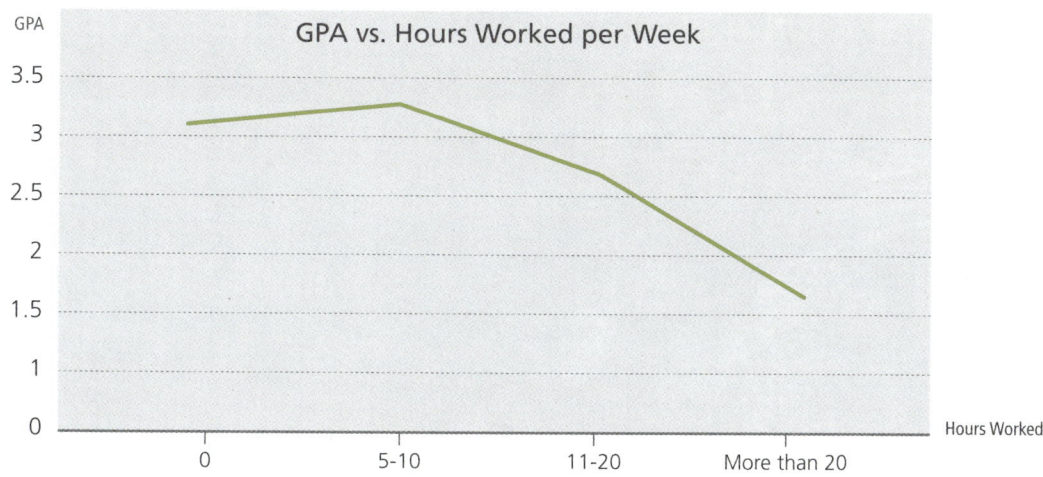

Work with a partner and answer the following questions. Phrases have been provided to help you.

1 Which group has the highest average GPA?

→ *The group with the highest average GPA is* _____.

2 Which group has the lowest average GPA?

→ *The group with the lowest average GPA is* _____.

3 Why do you think the average GPA of students who work more than 20 hours a week is so much lower than the other groups?

→ *I think this is due to* _____.

4 What is the overall message of this chart?

→ *The overall message of this chart is* _____.

Your Research

Find an article about part-time jobs for teenagers from a magazine, newspaper, or academic website. Paste or tape the article in your workbook in the space below.

Read your article and write four specific examples or pieces of evidence you can use for your debate. Try to include different types of examples, including opinion polls, statistics, academic studies, and general facts.

- _____
- _____
- _____
- _____

Debate Note-Taking

Use this page to take notes about the opposing team's arguments during the debate.

Note-Taking

Peer Evaluation

Read the assessment criteria and objectively evaluate your peers on a scale from 1 to 10.

CRITERIA	Name				
Understands the subject well	/10	/10	/10	/10	/10
Supports opinion with clear logic and examples	/10	/10	/10	/10	/10
Introduces opinions with appropriate connectors (In my view, I agree, For example, etc.)	/10	/10	/10	/10	/10
Uses a variety of vocabulary and expressions	/10	/10	/10	/10	/10
Accurately uses a variety of grammatical structures	/10	/10	/10	/10	/10
Does not monopolize the conversation and lets other people express themselves	/10	/10	/10	/10	/10
Listens attentively and respects other people's opinions	/10	/10	/10	/10	/10
Is able to accept criticism without becoming upset	/10	/10	/10	/10	/10
TOTAL SCORE	/80	/80	/80	/80	/80

Unit 03 Teaching Practical Subjects

Organizing Ideas

Should students learn more practical subjects at school?

Look at the reading passage in your textbook. List all the supporting arguments both FOR and AGAINST. Then, add the supporting logic and examples for each argument.

FOR	AGAINST
Argument 1	**Argument 1**
Support	**Support**
Argument 2	**Argument 2**
Support	**Support**
Argument 3	**Argument 3**
Support	**Support**

Making Supporting Examples: Academic Studies

Academic studies are research that is done by universities, governments, and large research organizations. During these studies, researchers examine events to understand what causes them and why they are important. Using academic studies is a good way to strengthen your argument. Below are some academic studies related to the topic of teaching practical subjects at school.

Additional Research

Before starting your argument, let's do some extra research on the topic. Read the academic study about teaching practical subjects at school.

Recently, some educators have started to question the value of studying traditional subjects such as literature and history. At the same time, a number of employers have complained that high school and college graduates lack the basic skills to do their jobs properly. Based on these points, this study will examine the value of teaching more practical subjects at schools and whether such a change is worth doing.

Few Schools Teach Practical Skills

A common complaint among employers is the lack of practical skills among their newly hired, recently graduated employees. Among their main concerns are the inability of new hires to write professional emails and documents, to read and understand their paystubs, and to make presentations. Our research has revealed that few schools adequately teach the above skills under their current curricula.

Challenges in Teaching Practical Skills

Part of the reason that few schools teach practical skills is that only a small number of them have teachers qualified to teach these subjects. By our estimates, a school of 1,000 students would have to hire approximately 8 new teachers to instruct students on subjects such as business writing, money management, and social skills for work environments. The situation is not likely to improve as many school districts are facing budget cuts.

Work with a partner and answer the following questions. Phrases have been provided to help you.

1 What are many employers complaining about?
 → *Employers are complaining about* _____.

2 What skills do recent graduates lack?
 → *Recent graduates lack skills such as* _____.

3 How many teachers to teach practical skills would a school of 500 students have to hire?
 → *The number of teachers it would need is* _____.

4 Why is it unlikely that schools will hire more teachers to teach practical skills?
 → *It is unlikely because* _____.

Your Research

Find an article about teaching practical subjects from a magazine, newspaper, or academic website. Paste or tape the article in your workbook in the space below.

Read your article and write four specific examples or pieces of evidence you can use for your debate. Try to include different types of examples, including opinion polls, statistics, academic studies, and general facts.

- _____
- _____
- _____
- _____

Debate Note-Taking

Use this page to take notes about the opposing team's arguments during the debate.

Note-Taking

Peer Evaluation

Read the assessment criteria and objectively evaluate your peers on a scale from 1 to 10.

CRITERIA	Name				
Understands the subject well	/10	/10	/10	/10	/10
Supports opinion with clear logic and examples	/10	/10	/10	/10	/10
Introduces opinions with appropriate connectors (In my view, I agree, For example, etc.)	/10	/10	/10	/10	/10
Uses a variety of vocabulary and expressions	/10	/10	/10	/10	/10
Accurately uses a variety of grammatical structures	/10	/10	/10	/10	/10
Does not monopolize the conversation and lets other people express themselves	/10	/10	/10	/10	/10
Listens attentively and respects other people's opinions	/10	/10	/10	/10	/10
Is able to accept criticism without becoming upset	/10	/10	/10	/10	/10
TOTAL SCORE	/80	/80	/80	/80	/80

Unit 04 Child Curfews

Organizing Ideas

Should governments make curfew laws for children?

Look at the reading passage in your textbook. List all the supporting arguments both FOR and AGAINST. Then, add the supporting logic and examples for each argument.

FOR	AGAINST
Argument 1	**Argument 1**
Support	**Support**
Argument 2	**Argument 2**
Support	**Support**
Argument 3	**Argument 3**
Support	**Support**

Making Supporting Examples: Personal Experience

Personal experience is your experience related to the topic. Using personal experience can be a good way to support your argument if you explain how your experience proves your point. However, you should be careful because one person's experience might not be common. This can actually weaken your argument. Below are some personal experiences related to the topic of child curfews.

Additional Research

Before starting your argument, let's do some extra research on the topic. Read the personal experiences about child curfews.

Kevin Wang, middle school student

I think child curfews are a silly idea. My friends and I often stay out after 10 at night, but it's not like we are causing trouble. Most of the time, we are just going back home after our academies finish. Sometimes, we hang out a bit at a fast-food restaurant and joke around. It's our way of relaxing after a hard day of studying. But if there were a child curfew, then we couldn't do this anymore. We would have to go home right away. That would be terrible. If lawmakers really want to make communities safer, then they should hire more police and track down serious lawbreakers, not a bunch of teenagers just having fun.

Yoonji Choi, sixth-grade student

This year, my city started a child curfew. My parents said it was to help keep kids safer. So far, I think the curfew is working well. In my case, I never need to go out by myself at night, and I don't see why any other kids would have to either. The only kids who would be out that late at night would probably be up to no good. For instance, some boys from my school got in trouble last year for spray painting some walls at night. Since there is a curfew, it is really easy for the police to keep these bad kids off the street. Any kid who is out is told to go home, where that person will be safe and can stay out of trouble. How easy is that?

Work with a partner and answer the following questions. Phrases have been provided to help you.

1 What does Kevin do when he is out after 10 PM?

→ *He usually* _____.

2 What solution does Kevin offer to make communities safer?

→ *His suggestion is* _____.

3 What happened to some boys from Yoonji's school?

→ *Some boys from her school* _____.

4 How do child curfews help the police according to Yoonji?

→ *They are helpful because* _____.

Your Research

Find an article about child curfews from a magazine, newspaper, or academic website. Paste or tape the article in your workbook in the space below.

Read your article and write four specific examples or pieces of evidence you can use for your debate. Try to include different types of examples, including opinion polls, statistics, academic studies, and general facts.

- _____
  _____
- _____
  _____
- _____
  _____
- _____
  _____

Debate Note-Taking

Use this page to take notes about the opposing team's arguments during the debate.

Note-Taking

_____
_____
_____
_____
_____
_____
_____
_____
_____
_____
_____

Peer Evaluation

Read the assessment criteria and objectively evaluate your peers on a scale from 1 to 10.

CRITERIA	Name				
Understands the subject well	/10	/10	/10	/10	/10
Supports opinion with clear logic and examples	/10	/10	/10	/10	/10
Introduces opinions with appropriate connectors (In my view, I agree, For example, etc.)	/10	/10	/10	/10	/10
Uses a variety of vocabulary and expressions	/10	/10	/10	/10	/10
Accurately uses a variety of grammatical structures	/10	/10	/10	/10	/10
Does not monopolize the conversation and lets other people express themselves	/10	/10	/10	/10	/10
Listens attentively and respects other people's opinions	/10	/10	/10	/10	/10
Is able to accept criticism without becoming upset	/10	/10	/10	/10	/10
TOTAL SCORE	/80	/80	/80	/80	/80

Unit 05 Internet Censorship

Organizing Ideas

Should governments be allowed to censor the Internet?

Look at the reading passage in your textbook. List all the supporting arguments both FOR and AGAINST. Then, add the supporting logic and examples for each argument.

FOR	AGAINST
Argument 1	**Argument 1**
Support	**Support**
Argument 2	**Argument 2**
Support	**Support**
Argument 3	**Argument 3**
Support	**Support**

22

Making Supporting Examples: Facts

A fact is something true. For debates, you can use facts that are common knowledge, but you should also try to use more specific, less commonly known facts. The best places to find specific facts are newspaper and magazine articles. In these sources, you can find all the details of a situation and can read interviews from people related to the story. Below are some facts related to the topic of Internet censorship.

Additional Research

Before starting your argument, let's do some extra research on the topic. Read the facts about Internet censorship.

> The country that has the most Internet censorship in the world is China. While the Internet remains mostly free in most other places, the time may not be far away when other countries start blocking content online. Here are some of the more shocking facts about Internet censorship in China:
>
> - **The Internet Police:** The Chinese government employs around 30,000 people to police the Internet. Their job is to track and arrest people who criticize the Chinese government online.
>
> - **Keystroke Recording:** Any time someone uses the Internet in China, each key that person presses is recorded. This means that the government can read what people type online, even private information such as personal emails.
>
> - **Blocked Websites:** Many of the world's most popular websites, including Facebook, YouTube, and Twitter, are blocked or heavily restricted in China. The reason is that the government does not want its people to access "unauthorized" information.
>
> - **Censorship of Information:** Any news stories and information critical of the Chinese government are censored. Only "good" news is allowed to be put online.

Work with a partner and answer the following questions. Phrases have been provided to help you.

1 What is the job of the Internet police in China?

→ *The Internet police are supposed to* _____ .

2 How does keystroke recording violate personal privacy?

→ *It violates personal privacy because* _____ .

3 Why does the Chinese government block websites such as Facebook?

→ *It blocks these sites because* _____ .

4 What type of information does the government in China censor?

→ *The government usually censors* _____ .

Your Research

Find an article about Internet censorship from a magazine, newspaper, or academic website. Paste or tape the article in your workbook in the space below.

Read your article and write four specific examples or pieces of evidence you can use for your debate. Try to include different types of examples, including opinion polls, statistics, academic studies, and general facts.

- _____
- _____
- _____
- _____

Debate Note-Taking

Use this page to take notes about the opposing team's arguments during the debate.

Note-Taking

Peer Evaluation

Read the assessment criteria and objectively evaluate your peers on a scale from 1 to 10.

CRITERIA	Name				
Understands the subject well	/10	/10	/10	/10	/10
Supports opinion with clear logic and examples	/10	/10	/10	/10	/10
Introduces opinions with appropriate connectors (In my view, I agree, For example, etc.)	/10	/10	/10	/10	/10
Uses a variety of vocabulary and expressions	/10	/10	/10	/10	/10
Accurately uses a variety of grammatical structures	/10	/10	/10	/10	/10
Does not monopolize the conversation and lets other people express themselves	/10	/10	/10	/10	/10
Listens attentively and respects other people's opinions	/10	/10	/10	/10	/10
Is able to accept criticism without becoming upset	/10	/10	/10	/10	/10
TOTAL SCORE	/80	/80	/80	/80	/80

Unit 06 Free Public Transportation

Organizing Ideas

Should people not have to pay to use public transportation?

Look at the reading passage in your textbook. List all the supporting arguments both FOR and AGAINST. Then, add the supporting logic and examples for each argument.

FOR

Argument 1
_____
_____
_____

Support
_____
_____
_____

Argument 2
_____
_____
_____

Support
_____
_____
_____

Argument 3
_____
_____
_____

Support
_____
_____
_____

AGAINST

Argument 1
_____
_____
_____

Support
_____
_____
_____

Argument 2
_____
_____
_____

Support
_____
_____
_____

Argument 3
_____
_____
_____

Support
_____
_____
_____

Making Supporting Examples: Academic Studies

Academic studies are research that is done by universities, governments, and large research organizations. During these studies, researchers examine events to understand what causes them and why they are important. Using academic studies is a good way to strengthen your argument. Below are some academic studies related to the topic of free public transportation.

Additional Research

Before starting your argument, let's do some extra research on the topic. Read the academic study about free public transportation.

> Cities around the world are looking for ways to reduce traffic congestion. The most commonly proposed solution is to make public transportation free to use. To see the effects of free public transportation, we have examined changes in ridership before and after its introduction.
>
> **Riders Respond More to Higher Prices than Lower Prices**
> Countless studies since the 1950s have found that riders respond much more strongly to increases in public transportation fares. Specifically, a fare increase of 25 percent reduces the number of riders significantly, often between 7 and 12 percent. On the other hand, a fare decrease by the same amount usually only increases ridership by less than 1 percent.
>
> **Free Public Transportation Not the Solution**
> Our data show that free public transportation has little effect on overall ridership. People who need to take public transportation to work generally do so regardless of the cost. Likewise, most drivers continue to use their cars even with no-cost public transportation. The most significant increase in ridership is among children and teenagers who are wasting time and space on public transportation. We have therefore concluded that cities would have to create disincentives for driving, such as raising car taxes and gas prices, for more people to use public transportation.

Work with a partner and answer the following questions. Phrases have been provided to help you.

1 By how much does a fare increase of 25 percent reduce the percentage of riders?
   → *The amount of riders is reduced by* _____.

2 What effect does a fare decrease by the same amount have?
   → *The effect is* _____.

3 How does offering free public transportation affect car drivers?
   → *Studies show that car drivers* _____.

4 What can cities do to encourage more people to use public transportation?
   → *The solution for cities is to* _____.

Your Research

Find an article about free public transportation from a magazine, newspaper, or academic website. Paste or tape the article in your workbook in the space below.

Read your article and write four specific examples or pieces of evidence you can use for your debate. Try to include different types of examples, including opinion polls, statistics, academic studies, and general facts.

- _____
  _____
- _____
  _____
- _____
  _____
- _____
  _____

Debate Note-Taking

Use this page to take notes about the opposing team's arguments during the debate.

Note-Taking

_____
_____
_____
_____
_____
_____
_____
_____
_____
_____
_____

Peer Evaluation

Read the assessment criteria and objectively evaluate your peers on a scale from 1 to 10.

CRITERIA	Name				
Understands the subject well	/10	/10	/10	/10	/10
Supports opinion with clear logic and examples	/10	/10	/10	/10	/10
Introduces opinions with appropriate connectors (In my view, I agree, For example, etc.)	/10	/10	/10	/10	/10
Uses a variety of vocabulary and expressions	/10	/10	/10	/10	/10
Accurately uses a variety of grammatical structures	/10	/10	/10	/10	/10
Does not monopolize the conversation and lets other people express themselves	/10	/10	/10	/10	/10
Listens attentively and respects other people's opinions	/10	/10	/10	/10	/10
Is able to accept criticism without becoming upset	/10	/10	/10	/10	/10
TOTAL SCORE	/80	/80	/80	/80	/80

Unit 07 Punishing Parents

Organizing Ideas

Should parents be punished when their children misbehave?

Look at the reading passage in your textbook. List all the supporting arguments both FOR and AGAINST. Then, add the supporting logic and examples for each argument.

FOR

Argument 1
_____
_____
_____

Support
_____
_____
_____

Argument 2
_____
_____
_____

Support
_____
_____
_____

Argument 3
_____
_____
_____

Support
_____
_____
_____

AGAINST

Argument 1
_____
_____
_____

Support
_____
_____
_____

Argument 2
_____
_____
_____

Support
_____
_____
_____

Argument 3
_____
_____
_____

Support
_____
_____
_____

Making Supporting Examples: Facts

A fact is something true. For debates, you can use facts that are common knowledge, but you should also try to use more specific, less commonly known facts. The best places to find specific facts are newspaper and magazine articles. In these sources, you can find all the details of a situation and can read interviews from people related to the story. Below are some facts related to the topic of punishing parents.

Additional Research

Before starting your argument, let's do some extra research on the topic. Read the facts about punishing parents.

> Why are children today causing problems at school? If you look at the facts, you will see that the children are not at fault, but the parents are! Here are some ways that parents are encouraging bad behavior at school:
>
> - A majority of parents are afraid to discipline their children. Many parents feel it is better to be friendly to their children. The problem with this is that children will lose respect for their parents and therefore behave badly.
> - Another problem is that many parents fail to keep their discipline promises. By not keeping their promises, children learn that they can break the rules without being properly punished. This allows bad behavior to continue.
> - A growing number of parents side with their children when their teachers punish them at school. This weakens the power of teachers as disciplinarians and puts children in a position of too much power.
> - Many parents rely on technology such as smartphones and video games to keep their children occupied rather than spending time with their children.

Work with a partner and answer the following questions. Phrases have been provided to help you.

1 What problem happens when parents act friendly to their children?
   → *The main problem is* _____.

2 If parents do not keep their punishment promises, how do children respond?
   → *Children respond by* _____.

3 How does poor parenting weaken the authority of teachers?
   → *It can lead to* _____.

4 Why is the problem caused by technology?
   → *The problem with technology is* _____.

Your Research

Find an article about punishing parents for their children's misbehavior from a magazine, newspaper, or academic website. Paste or tape the article in your workbook in the space below.

Paste or Tape Your Research Article Here

Read your article and write four specific examples or pieces of evidence you can use for your debate. Try to include different types of examples, including opinion polls, statistics, academic studies, and general facts.

- _____
- _____
- _____
- _____

Debate Note-Taking

Use this page to take notes about the opposing team's arguments during the debate.

Note-Taking

_____
_____
_____
_____
_____
_____
_____
_____
_____
_____
_____
_____

Peer Evaluation

Read the assessment criteria and objectively evaluate your peers on a scale from 1 to 10.

CRITERIA	Name				
Understands the subject well	/10	/10	/10	/10	/10
Supports opinion with clear logic and examples	/10	/10	/10	/10	/10
Introduces opinions with appropriate connectors (In my view, I agree, For example, etc.)	/10	/10	/10	/10	/10
Uses a variety of vocabulary and expressions	/10	/10	/10	/10	/10
Accurately uses a variety of grammatical structures	/10	/10	/10	/10	/10
Does not monopolize the conversation and lets other people express themselves	/10	/10	/10	/10	/10
Listens attentively and respects other people's opinions	/10	/10	/10	/10	/10
Is able to accept criticism without becoming upset	/10	/10	/10	/10	/10
TOTAL SCORE	/80	/80	/80	/80	/80

Unit 08: Studying Abroad

Organizing Ideas

Should children study abroad away from their families?

Look at the reading passage in your textbook. List all the supporting arguments both FOR and AGAINST. Then, add the supporting logic and examples for each argument.

FOR	AGAINST
Argument 1	**Argument 1**
Support	**Support**
Argument 2	**Argument 2**
Support	**Support**
Argument 3	**Argument 3**
Support	**Support**

Making Supporting Examples: Personal Experience

Personal experience is your experience related to the topic. Using personal experience can be a good way to support your argument if you explain how your experience proves your point. However, you should be careful because one person's experience might not be common. This can actually weaken your argument. Below are some personal experiences related to the topic of studying abroad.

Additional Research

Before starting your argument, let's do some extra research on the topic. Read the personal experiences about studying abroad.

Dongbin Yang, eighth-grade student

I regret not studying abroad when I had the chance. When I was in the fourth grade, my parents asked me if I wanted to go school in America. Since I was just a little kid, I didn't think about the benefits of moving to the U.S. I just thought about how much I would miss my friends at school, so I told them no. That was a mistake. A lot of my friends at school have lived abroad, and they told me about their experiences. They said they really enjoyed living in another culture, and they all speak English fluently. Any drawbacks to studying abroad are certainly outweighed by the benefits.

Miho Watanabe, seventh-grade student

I lived abroad in New Zealand for two years during elementary school. It was one of the hardest times of my life. I had to leave all of my friends and most of my family behind in Japan when I went abroad. The hardest part was learning English. When I went to New Zealand, I didn't speak English well at all, so some of the kids at the New Zealand school made fun of my speaking. But even worse, I had a lot of trouble understanding my schoolwork. So I spent most of my first year having a hard time at school and had few friends. The second year was better, but I missed being home in Japan. All in all, I think it would have been for me just to stay home.

Work with a partner and answer the following questions. Phrases have been provided to help you.

1 Why did Dongbin choose not to study abroad?
   → *He did not study abroad because* _____.

2 What do Dongbin's friends think about their experiences studying abroad?
   → *His friends think that* _____.

3 Why did some of the students at Miho's school in New Zealand make fun of her?
   → *The students made fun of her because* _____.

4 How does Miho feel about her experience overall?
   → *Overall, she feels that* _____.

Your Research

Find an article about children studying abroad from a magazine, newspaper, or academic website. Paste or tape the article in your workbook in the space below.

Paste or Tape Your Research Article Here

Read your article and write four specific examples or pieces of evidence you can use for your debate. Try to include different types of examples, including opinion polls, statistics, academic studies, and general facts.

- _____
- _____
- _____
- _____

Debate Note-Taking

Use this page to take notes about the opposing team's arguments during the debate.

Note-Taking

_____
_____
_____
_____
_____
_____
_____
_____
_____
_____
_____
_____

Peer Evaluation

Read the assessment criteria and objectively evaluate your peers on a scale from 1 to 10.

CRITERIA	Name				
Understands the subject well	/10	/10	/10	/10	/10
Supports opinion with clear logic and examples	/10	/10	/10	/10	/10
Introduces opinions with appropriate connectors (In my view, I agree, For example, etc.)	/10	/10	/10	/10	/10
Uses a variety of vocabulary and expressions	/10	/10	/10	/10	/10
Accurately uses a variety of grammatical structures	/10	/10	/10	/10	/10
Does not monopolize the conversation and lets other people express themselves	/10	/10	/10	/10	/10
Listens attentively and respects other people's opinions	/10	/10	/10	/10	/10
Is able to accept criticism without becoming upset	/10	/10	/10	/10	/10
TOTAL SCORE	/80	/80	/80	/80	/80

Unit 09: Universal Healthcare

Organizing Ideas

Should governments provide healthcare to all of their citizens?

Look at the reading passage in your textbook. List all the supporting arguments both FOR and AGAINST. Then, add the supporting logic and examples for each argument.

FOR	AGAINST
Argument 1	**Argument 1**
Support	**Support**
Argument 2	**Argument 2**
Support	**Support**
Argument 3	**Argument 3**
Support	**Support**

Making Supporting Examples: Expert Opinions

Expert opinions are usually the ideas and opinions of experts in any given field. Experts are typically people such as professors, doctors, and business managers. Most experts base their opinions on their years of experience doing research and working in their fields. Below are some expert opinions related to the topic of universal healthcare.

Additional Research

Before starting your argument, let's do some extra research on the topic. Read the expert opinions about universal healthcare.

Edward Douglas, Director of California Department of Healthcare Services

Over 20 percent of the nearly 40 million residents of California have little to no healthcare coverage. Without insurance, most of these people cannot get even routine checkups at the doctor's office. Remember that one visit to the doctor's costs $100 or more, and that's not including the price of medicine. What's the solution? Free healthcare for all, or at least for those who need it most. The U.S. government already spends more than 18 percent of the national income on healthcare while countries that offer universal healthcare all spend around just 10 percent of their budgets. Money is not an issue. Creating a system that works is.

Jennifer Conrad, National Health Department Manager

The concept of universal healthcare is good. In practice, however, it has major shortcomings. The biggest problem with universal healthcare is not cost, but quality. Attracting the most talented doctors requires paying high salaries. Under free healthcare, there is a good chance that doctor's salaries would decrease. With this decrease, the talent of our medical professionals would also go down. In addition, free healthcare would lead to extreme demand for medical treatment. Our nation's already crowded hospitals would be filled beyond their capacity to treat people. This would mean longer waits and even lower quality service.

Work with a partner and answer the following questions. Phrases have been provided to help you.

1 How many people in California do not have proper healthcare?

→ *The number of people is* _____.

2 What percent of the national budget does the United States government spend on healthcare? What about other countries?

→ *The U.S. government spends* _____

while other governments _____.

3 According to Jennifer Conrad, what is the main shortcoming of free healthcare?

→ *She says the main shortcoming is* _____.

4 How would hospitals be affected by free healthcare?

→ *Hospitals would* _____.

Your Research

Find an article about universal healthcare from a magazine, newspaper, or academic website. Paste or tape the article in your workbook in the space below.

Paste or Tape Your Research Article Here

Read your article and write four specific examples or pieces of evidence you can use for your debate. Try to include different types of examples, including opinion polls, statistics, academic studies, and general facts.

- _____
- _____
- _____
- _____

Debate Note-Taking

Use this page to take notes about the opposing team's arguments during the debate.

Note-Taking

_____
_____
_____
_____
_____
_____
_____
_____
_____
_____
_____
_____

Peer Evaluation

Read the assessment criteria and objectively evaluate your peers on a scale from 1 to 10.

CRITERIA	Name				
Understands the subject well	/10	/10	/10	/10	/10
Supports opinion with clear logic and examples	/10	/10	/10	/10	/10
Introduces opinions with appropriate connectors (In my view, I agree, For example, etc.)	/10	/10	/10	/10	/10
Uses a variety of vocabulary and expressions	/10	/10	/10	/10	/10
Accurately uses a variety of grammatical structures	/10	/10	/10	/10	/10
Does not monopolize the conversation and lets other people express themselves	/10	/10	/10	/10	/10
Listens attentively and respects other people's opinions	/10	/10	/10	/10	/10
Is able to accept criticism without becoming upset	/10	/10	/10	/10	/10
TOTAL SCORE	/80	/80	/80	/80	/80

Unit 10 Nuclear Weapons

Organizing Ideas

Should nations be allowed to keep nuclear weapons?

Look at the reading passage in your textbook. List all the supporting arguments both FOR and AGAINST. Then, add the supporting logic and examples for each argument.

FOR	AGAINST
Argument 1	**Argument 1**
Support	**Support**
Argument 2	**Argument 2**
Support	**Support**
Argument 3	**Argument 3**
Support	**Support**

Making Supporting Examples: Statistics

Statistics are facts based on numbers. They are usually created by governments, universities, news organizations, and companies. Statistics often show the number of people, companies, and nations that agree with a certain opinion or policy. To show these numbers, statistics can include percentages, populations, and points. Below are some statistics related to the topic of nuclear weapons.

Additional Research

Before starting your argument, let's do some extra research on the topic. Read the statistics on nuclear weapons.

Nuclear Weapons during World War II

- The top-secret Manhattan Project in 1945, created to develop the first nuclear weapons, cost $20 billion. This was about 7 percent of the entire cost of World War II.
- The atomic bomb dropped on Hiroshima weighed 15 kilotons and destroyed 13 square kilometers of the city. All people within one kilometer of the blast were killed instantly, and 92 percent of the structures were destroyed. In total, 200,000 people died from the explosion and exposure to raditation.

Nuclear Weapons Today

- Currently, there are 26,000 nuclear weapons in the world. This is enough to kill everyone of the planent several times over.
- Today's nuclear weapons are much more powerful than the ones dropped on Japan. It is estimated that just one of today's atomic bombs could kill 4,000,000 people.
- The United States spends around $40 billion dollars a year to produce nuclear weapons. This is enough money to provide universal healthcare, education, food, and clean water supplies to everybody in the world.

Work with a partner and answer the following questions. Phrases have been provided to help you.

1 How much did it cost to develop the nuclear weapons used during World War II?

→ *The total cost of the Manhattan Project was* _____.

2 What was the destructive power of the atomic bomb dropped on Hiroshima?

→ *The power of that bomb was* _____.

3 How many times more deadly is one of today's nuclear weapons compared to the ones dropped on Japan?

→ *Modern bombs are* _____.

4 What is the overall message of these statistics?

→ *The overall message of these statistics is that* _____.

Your Research

Find an article about nuclear weapons from a magazine, newspaper, or academic website. Paste or tape the article in your workbook in the space below.

Read your article and write four specific examples or pieces of evidence you can use for your debate. Try to include different types of examples, including opinion polls, statistics, academic studies, and general facts.

- _____
  _____
- _____
  _____
- _____
  _____
- _____
  _____

Debate Note-Taking

Use this page to take notes about the opposing team's arguments during the debate.

Note-Taking

_____
_____
_____
_____
_____
_____
_____
_____
_____
_____
_____
_____

Peer Evaluation

Read the assessment criteria and objectively evaluate your peers on a scale from 1 to 10.

CRITERIA	Name				
Understands the subject well	/10	/10	/10	/10	/10
Supports opinion with clear logic and examples	/10	/10	/10	/10	/10
Introduces opinions with appropriate connectors (In my view, I agree, For example, etc.)	/10	/10	/10	/10	/10
Uses a variety of vocabulary and expressions	/10	/10	/10	/10	/10
Accurately uses a variety of grammatical structures	/10	/10	/10	/10	/10
Does not monopolize the conversation and lets other people express themselves	/10	/10	/10	/10	/10
Listens attentively and respects other people's opinions	/10	/10	/10	/10	/10
Is able to accept criticism without becoming upset	/10	/10	/10	/10	/10
TOTAL SCORE	/80	/80	/80	/80	/80

Memo

Memo

DEBATE Pro
Book 4

Workbook